New Directions for
Child and Adolescent
Development

Reed W. Larson
Lene Arnett Jensen
EDITORS-IN-CHIEF

William Damon
FOUNDING EDITOR

W9-AVQ-027

New Horizons in Developmental Theory and Research

Lene Arnett Jensen
Reed W. Larson
EDITORS

Number 109 • Fall 2005
Jossey-Bass
San Francisco

New Horizons in Developmental Theory and Research
Lene Arnett Jensen, Reed W. Larson (eds.)
New Directions for Child and Adolescent Development, no. 109
William Damon, Editor-in-Chief

Microfilm copies of issues and articles are available in 16mm and 35mm, as well as microfiche in 105mm, through University Microfilms Inc., 300 North Zeeb Road, Ann Arbor, Michigan 48106-1346.

ISSN 1520-3247   electronic ISSN 1534-8687

NEW DIRECTIONS FOR CHILD AND ADOLESCENT DEVELOPMENT is part of The Jossey-Bass Education Series and is published quarterly by Wiley Subscription Services, Inc., a Wiley company, at Jossey-Bass, 989 Market Street, San Francisco, California 94103-1741. Periodicals postage paid at San Francisco, California, and at additional mailing offices. Postmaster: Send address changes to New Directions for Child and Adolescent Development, Jossey-Bass, 989 Market Street, San Francisco, CA 94103-1741.

New Directions for Child and Adolescent Development is indexed in Biosciences Information Service, Current Index to Journals in Education (ERIC), Psychological Abstracts, and Sociological Abstracts.

SUBSCRIPTIONS cost $90.00 for individuals and $205.00 for institutions, agencies, and libraries.

EDITORIAL CORRESPONDENCE should be sent to the Editor-in-Chief, William Damon, Stanford Center on Adolescence, Cypress Building C, Stanford University, Stanford, CA 94305.

Jossey-Bass Web address: www.josseybass.com

CONTENTS

A MESSAGE FROM THE NEW EDITORS-IN-CHIEF

When we had our first conversation with Bill Damon about taking over *New Directions for Child and Adolescent Development*, we were struck by one of the words he used to describe his vision for the type of work it should publish: "edgy." We liked the word. Of course, it suggests "cutting edge" (although that is a quality that can be conclusively judged only in retrospect). Or it might mean "near the edge," invoking a fall into a precipice if one took a step further. Edgy is also a synonym for anxiety, an emotional state one may feel in taking risks and not being quite sure where one's feet are planted. What we embrace in these meanings is the vision that a field grows when there are venues that permit exploration and development in new (sometimes risky) terrain.

The notion that this series is as much about ideas as empirical findings is another part of the vision that Bill passed on to us. For a field to be vital, it needs public spaces where concepts and theories can be developed and examined, even if the evidence to back these ideas is partial. The field of developmental science and scholarship strikes us, at times, as a clutter of cold facts and coefficients. Poincaré wrote, "Science is built up of facts, as a house is built of stones; but an accumulation of facts is no more a science than a heap of stones is a house." One more likely sees the "heap of stones" in Poincaré's famous quote than the house constructed with theory that he saw as the objective for science. To make a house from its stones, developmental science needs to continually explore new paradigms, challenge or revitalize old ones, pose profound questions, and develop hypotheses. For the study of humans, there is a particular imperative to conceptualize behavior in relationship to context and probe multiple levels of process and meaning.

Although there is less of an accepted canon for evaluating what makes for good ideas, especially edgy ones, we appeal to the standard family of criteria. Evidence is certainly important; we'd prefer to see an outline for a house that has some "stones" in it. New ideas are most compelling when research findings (quantitative, qualitative, lab experiments, and so on) have begun to demonstrate the empirical potential of the ideas. Usability and, dare we say, predictability are traits that add to the worth of ideas. In a cluttered world, parsimony, simplicity, and elegance are highly valued, especially ideas that integrate two or more topics. We place, closely related, a high value on ideas that are clearly communicated (we have already become a broken record in encouraging authors to have a good "hook" in their articles and good topic sentences for every paragraph). Yet another vital criterion is meaningfulness: good ideas are good because they address the "so what?" question.

One set of checks and balances against going too far over the edge, built into the format of *New Directions* volumes, is that the ideas being developed must be collective. The series publishes edited volumes in which multiple authors contribute. So if a new idea is folly, at least it must be collective folly. Our inclination is to look particularly favorably on proposals in which authors approach their shared new direction from divergent (even conflicting) vantage points. As two examples, we have upcoming volumes that look at family mealtime and positive female sexual development from diverse disciplinary perspectives. We also welcome proposals that use innovative formats for conversation, collaboration, or debate.

As should be clear by now, we do not want to define *a priori* boundaries on the type of developmental topic or approach that we will accept for publication. If you are considering something, send us an e-mail, and we will discuss it with you. (You may also obtain further information on the scope of the journal and how to submit a proposal for a volume at http://www3. interscience.wiley.com/cgi-bin/jhome/85511342.) The articles in this, our inaugural volume, represent a selection of the topics that we are interested in. We are eager to have *New Directions* explore a range of issues: poverty, education, infant development, community contexts, gene-environment interactions, ethnicity, research methods, epistemology, and numerous other topics.

In short, our objective is for the series to provide a healthy "developmental context" for the broad growth and development of the field. We encourage you to consider submitting a proposal to contribute to this process of expanding the horizons and "edges" of the field.

REED W. LARSON
LENE ARNETT JENSEN

PART ONE

Introductions

1

This volume brings together leading scholars to describe important new directions in research on child and adolescent development. This introductory chapter places their articles in the context of three larger trends in the field.

Developmental Horizons: Legacies and Prospects in Child and Adolescent Development

Lene Arnett Jensen, Reed W. Larson

The field of child and adolescent development has a short history, if we consider it to have originated with the Child Study movement of the late nineteenth century. But already in that time it has seen a number of shifts in theoretical directions. Each new theoretical approach has grappled with its own issues and left its own legacy. At the same time, every approach since then has also sought to answer a number of common questions: To what extent are children's and adolescents' development shaped by the culture in which they grow up? What are the most influential developmental contexts: parents, friends, media, or something else? How do children develop the capacity to control their thoughts, emotions, and behaviors? The aim in this introductory chapter is to survey future prospects for developmental theory and research addressing these common questions.

As the series itself takes a new direction with our assuming the editorship, we are delighted to present this first volume, which looks broadly at some of the new directions today in our field. The volume brings together a group of cutting-edge developmental scholars with diverse areas of expertise. We have arranged their chapters into three parts, pertaining to culture, developmental contexts, and emotional and cognitive self-regulation.

William Damon, the founding editor, starts the volume off in Chapter Two with retrospective reflections on the dramatic changes in the field since the start of the series in 1978. He concludes with a prediction and challenge: that an important horizon for the field is formulating theories

New Directions for Child and Adolescent Development, no. 109, Fall 2005 © Wiley Periodicals, Inc.

that integrate domains of developmental studies. Developing integrations of this type—between self and culture, development and context, emotion and cognition, among other things—is also an underlying theme across these diverse chapters.

Self-in-Culture

In recent years, the perspectives and analytic repertoire of developmental scholars have expanded. To the long-standing nomothetic and idiographic approaches to human development, we have added a cultural one. Now our descriptions and explanations of thought and behavior address not only human universals and individual uniqueness but also the diversity of peoples.

The cultural approach is not completely new to psychology. At various points since its founding, psychologists have cast an occasional glimpse at the role that culture plays in development. For example, in the 1860s Wilhelm Wundt formulated a program of "folk psychology" (*Völkerpsychologi* in German) to complement his far-better-known experimental psychology. Folk psychology was to be the study of how human mental processes develop in historical context, and Wundt produced a ten-volume work on the languages, myths, and customs of diverse cultures. G. Stanley Hall, one of Wundt's American followers, also incorporated information on cultural customs into his landmark 1904 volumes on adolescence. In Russia, Lev Vygotsky, in the 1920s and early 1930s, conceived of a developmental psychology that portrays the person in sociocultural context. However, these early flashes of attention to culture, along with others that followed, never consolidated into a coherent, full-fledged cultural approach.

Although most textbooks still do not give the cultural approach a place of its own next to the nomothetic and idiographic ones, there is no doubt that recent years have seen the ascent of such an approach in psychology. Today's world brings people of differing cultures into vastly more contact with one another in real and virtual space than did the worlds of Wundt, Hall, and Vygotsky. With this expansion in intercultural contact, developmental scholars too have expanded their perspective. Culture may not become the single most important construct of research in developmental psychology (as it is in the new area of cultural psychology), but the study of how culture intersects with development has become vital and is likely to remain so.

Travel has broadened our horizon, but we now need to ask "Where to next?" in researching how the self develops in culture. The four chapters in Part Two of this volume that are centrally concerned with this question offer a host of keen and constructive new insights. Collectively, they demonstrate that when we conduct research with culturally diverse groups we need to be wary of setting out with a suitcase already full of theories and methods developed for one group (often the American middle class). We need not leave with nothing, but there has to be room for discovering new and positive conceptions of developmental means, ends, transitions, and phases.

The need to conceptualize cultural groups in sophisticated and positive ways is a key refreshing message in Chapter Three, by Marcela Raffaelli, Gustavo Carlo, Miguel A. Carranza, and Gloria E. Gonzales-Kruger. Focusing on Latinos in the United States, they take as a starting observation the fact that currently 17 percent of American children and adolescents are Latino, and projections suggest that by 2050 this number will double. They point out that this sizeable sector of the U.S. population cannot be lumped together easily. Latino groups are highly diverse on factors such as immigration status, educational achievement, home language, household composition, and degree of acculturation, as well as nation and cultural group of origin. Future research needs to differentiate factors such as these. Raffaelli and her colleagues also call for a focus on positive development among Latino groups. The suggestion is not that we ignore problem behaviors but that we see them as one part of a much larger research agenda to develop a model of "Latino youth development." In addition to being important in its own right, the study of diverse Latino groups may open up a trove of valuable insights, for example on the positive functions of respect for elders and family connectedness.

Chapter Four, by Joan G. Miller, is a lucid elaboration on the need for future research to consider that children and adolescents who are members of different cultural groups grow up with diverse developmental aims. Miller surveys cross-cultural research in three areas: understanding of self and others, moral development, and attachment. For each area, she notes how work with children in such places as India, Japan, and Puerto Rico shines a light on psychological concepts to which American psychology has paid little or no attention. To preview just one of Miller's several thought-provoking examples, research has shown that as they grow older European American children and adolescents describe themselves and others increasingly in terms of such personality characteristics as extraverted, shy, and funny, whereas children and adolescents in India increasingly use role-based descriptors, such as daughter, mother, and uncle. Miller's central point is that children and adolescents across the globe are not headed toward one uniform set of psychological end goals. Her chapter also gives rise to complex questions regarding intercultural understanding. For example, how do developmental scholars (and people more generally) reconcile goals that may stand in some opposition to one another, such as individual authenticity and being dutiful, or independence and respect for elders?

T. S. Saraswathi (Chapter Five) adds new meaning to notions of independence and interdependence, and her chapter constitutes a fitting companion piece to Miller's. Saraswathi gives an account of how varying psychological goals are in focus during the four phases of the Hindu Indian conception of the life course. Fulfilling role-based obligations is at a premium during the first two phases of being a student and householder (as is also noted by Miller). A transcendental independence or release of the Hindu self, the "Atman," is at the heart of the next two phases, retirement and renunciation of society. The latter goal of release of the self, in particular, is outside mainstream Western psychology but clearly central to the lives of Hindu Indians—and undoubtedly people in other places as well. Saraswathi suggests a future research program where the phases of the life course are placed in a cultural context.

If the end goals of developmental phases vary cross-culturally, it should not be surprising if developmental processes—the means to the goals—also vary cross-culturally. What may be more surprising, however, is how these processes involve everyday events that are habitual and routine. According to Peggy J. Miller and Sarah C. Mangelsdorf (Chapter Six), one of these everyday events is personal storytelling, particularly stories in which children hear their actions recounted. In their eloquent chapter, they offer a new integration of research on attachment and cross-cultural research on communication. They propose that in-depth understanding of the self requires focusing on how self-concepts develop out of social relationships and how those relationships routinely involve communication and narration pertaining to the self. Everywhere parents tell stories to and about their children, but which stories get told, when, to whom, and how they are told varies. Thus, Miller and Mangelsdorf write: "Wherever it occurs, personal storytelling takes on local color, absorbing values, affective stances, and moral orientations. As young children participate routinely in their community's version of personal storytelling, they learn to interpret their experiences in culture-specific terms, carving out culture-specific selves." Miller and Mangelsdorf focus on storytelling. However, their argument that everyday routines are far from mundane and instead reflect crucial cultural beliefs can easily apply to a host of other daily routines: sleeping arrangements, how infants are carried, cell phone use, meal times, and others.

Development-in-Contexts

Developmental research on the contexts of children's and adolescents' lives has gradually changed in two important respects, one quantitative and the other qualitative. The quantitative change is that we have greatly expanded the number of contexts that we address. The psychodynamic and behavioristic approaches that dominated the first half of the twentieth century focused on a limited number of contexts. Although holding highly divergent conceptions of the mechanisms involved in bringing about healthy and unhealthy psychological development, the two approaches shared a prominent focus on the role of the family context (especially parents) in children's lives. During the last few decades, however, developmental psychologists have addressed an increasing number of other contexts. This change is well exemplified in Bronfenbrenner's ecological approach, which in one fell theoretical swoop added myriad relationships, groups, and networks to the vista of developmental scholars. With the ecological approach came new attention to such contexts as day care, the legal system, and overarching cultural belief systems, as well as interconnections among these contexts. Even now, we are adding new contexts. For example, current developmental research increasingly examines media and after-school and community programs. The developmental field, then, has seen what we might term a "pluralization of contexts."

In addition to this quantitative change, an important qualitative change has occurred within the field. We have moved away from a one-way, top-down conception of how contexts form children and adolescents to a two-way conception that recognizes how children and adolescents also bring much into their contexts. Freud and Watson provided vivid accounts of how parents and other socialization agents influence children. They had less to say about how children influence their surroundings. Watson's famous and particularly strong statement—that if given "a dozen healthy infants . . . I'll guarantee to take any one at random and train him to become any type of specialist I might select"—sounds exaggerated to today's developmental scholars. Researchers now address how children and adolescents bring feelings, concepts, motives, and abilities to their contexts. A new perspective has emerged, then, that draws attention to contexts as being co-constructed.

In Part Three, we include chapters on four contexts that are prominent in the lives of today's children and adolescents. Two of these contexts, media and civic organizations, are of fairly recent interest to developmental scholars, whereas the other two, family and friends, have been of interest for a longer time. Taken together, the chapters highlight important thoughts and behaviors that children take from *and* bring to the contexts within which they develop.

The central message of L. Monique Ward's engaging Chapter Seven is that media have come to play a prominent and powerful part in the lives of children and adolescents. According to Ward, American children who are between eight and eighteen years old currently spend almost eight hours a day on media, watching TV, listening to music, playing video games, and using the Internet. To use the creative language of Ward's chapter title, all of this media use has serious implications for the "minds, bodies, and deeds" of contemporary children and adolescents. Drawing on a substantial body of interdisciplinary research, she argues that media influence deep-seated attitudes, feelings, and behaviors, notably body image, self-esteem, and sexual activities. Comparing Ward's chapter with Miller and Mangelsdorf's (Chapter Six), we might think of media as a form of public storytelling that, just like personal storytelling, has become routine with profound attendant influences on the self. Although Ward focuses principally on the path of influence from media to youth, other researchers have shown that these transactions also involve two-way processes, particularly in young people's engagement with new interactive media (Sharma, 2004).

James Youniss and Daniel Hart point to the favorable impact for both youth and society of adolescents' engagement in civic organizations. The authors of Chapter Eight describe several community programs where adolescents come together and, often in collaboration with adults, work toward common civic goals. Youniss and Hart also document how such successful youth civic engagement in part draws on psychological competencies that adolescents bring into the context and in part strengthens and fosters new competencies. On the basis of these and other research findings, Youniss and Hart draw out several perspicacious implications for future developmental research and social policy. At the center of these implications is a positive conception of adolescents as collaborative rather than solitary, creative rather than destructive, and purposeful rather than apathetic.

Jacqueline J. Goodnow, like Youniss and Hart, argues in Chapter Nine that socialization involves far more than children learning the lessons of older generations. Focusing on family, she observes that "psychologists . . . seem prone to see life as determined only by 'how the twig is bent,' and that proneness calls for closer analysis than it has so far received." Goodnow's point is twofold. She emphasizes that family socialization is important beyond the early, or "twig," phase of a child's life, and that family socialization involves learning not only agreement but also resistance, negotiation, and compromise in interacting with older generations. She calls for research that examines the extent to which these diverse socialization outcomes depend on factors such as the issue at hand (for example, household chores, calling a family member by first name, or doing school work), the person in question (a grandmother or a sibling), and the culture under investigation (for instance, whether more or less collectivistic). What Goodnow accomplishes in her chapter is to show how family—an entity of long-standing interest to developmental scholars—can be both a top-down and a bottom-up developmental context from infancy through adulthood.

Just as Goodnow challenges us to think about family in new terms, in Chapter Ten William M. Bukowski and Lorrie K. Sippola call for new paradigms in research on friendships. More precisely, they call for us to go "back to the future," to return to broader conceptions of "the stuff" of friendships envisioned by early theorists such as Harry Stack Sullivan. Although recent research has given much attention to the role of friendship in individual adjustment and well-being, Bukowski and Sippola argue for attention to wider basic processes, such as how friendships work day-to-day, the dynamic interface between self and other, and the provisions of friendship for satisfying human needs such as security. As a powerful example, they describe new studies showing how friendship can serve as a zone of comfort for identity exploration; however, it appears that this provision can only be used if one brings sufficient self-esteem into the friendship to be able to balance one's own and others' needs. Their proposed conception of friendship, then, presents it as a complex, active, two-way set of processes, which reflects the horizon of research we see across diverse developmental contexts.

Self-Regulation of Emotion and Cognition

One reason developmental scholars have moved toward a bidirectional conception of the relation between children and environmental contexts is the changes that have occurred in how we think about the intersection of biology and environment. The field has moved away from a long-standing emphasis on environmental determinism—epitomized by Watson and his conviction that he could make any infant in the image he chose—toward the view that children bring inherent characteristics or propensities to their interactions with parents, friends, teachers, media, and so forth. At the same time, however, the field is rejecting the opposite pendulum swing toward biological determinism, which has seen personality traits as hard-wired and genes as exerting a fixed influence on behavioral development. Defining the middle ground between these views, a recent national panel of leading researchers concluded that the development of children unfolds along "individual pathways" shaped by the ongoing interaction of biology, daily environments, and children' active participation in these environments (National Research Council and Institute of Medicine, 2002).

Chapters Eleven, Twelve, and Thirteen here speak to how these complex interactions shape pathways for the development of self-regulation, which this same national panel concluded "is a cornerstone of early childhood development" (p. 3). The goals of the work described in the three chapters of Part Four are diverse, including understanding the components of the pathways that are shared across children as well as those that vary between individual children. They also include creating environments that can compensate for individual developmental risks and enhance positive inherent dispositions in children and adolescents. The three chapters included here on regulation of emotion and cognition detail some of this latest research and propose new theoretical models to guide future research in this area.

Mary K. Rothbart and Michael I. Posner in Chapter Eleven give a thought-provoking account of their newest research, addressing the development of effortful control in terms of interconnections between genes, neural networks, and environmental interventions. Rothbart and Posner conceptualize effortful control as the ability "to inhibit a dominant response in order to perform a subdominant response, detect errors, and engage in planning." They argue that temperamental differences exist between individuals in their capacity for effortful control, but environment and experience as well can substantially influence the development of this capacity. Indeed, their recent experiments have found that participation in a five-day program increased four-year-old children's performance on tasks requiring effortful control and showed changes in their EEG patterns consistent with improved effortful control. The horizon Rothbart and Posner point to for this research includes identifying genotypic variations among children that influence these developmental pathways, and development of training programs in preschool that assist children's growth in the ability to self-regulate.

Designing intervention programs to enhance children's self-regulation is also an important potential future application of the impressive research models that Nancy Eisenberg, Adrienne Sadovsky, and Tracy L. Spinrad propose in Chapter Twelve. They focus on "emotion-related regulation," a concept that includes a range of abilities for self-control, notably inhibition and activation of behavior, planning, attention, and the ability to influence the environment. Their chapter pulls together extensive research to propose two heuristic models for understanding the development of this capacity in relationship to other developing competencies, knowledge, and dispositions. Their first model proposes a set of early developmental influences among emotion regulation, language skills, and emotion knowledge. The second model suggests how these factors are associated with academic motivation and competence as children enter school. These heuristic models furnish a roadmap for future research and suggest the range of interacting factors that must be considered in planning interventions for children at different ages.

Mary Gauvain focuses on cognitive development; her Chapter Thirteen also addresses themes regarding pathways in the development of self-regulation. She begins by tracing a thirty-year history of cognitive development to show how the area has grown, and in turn she proposes three promising new research directions. One involves work on the biology of cognitive development; she points to new work aimed at understanding how emotional systems and emotional regulation influence cognitive growth. An interesting point she adds to the two preceding chapters of Part Four highlights the role of parents in adjusting emotional conditions to the temperament of the child so as to facilitate the child's cognitive development. Her second topic is research on learning; she describes new work on problem solving and strategy development, domains of growth that also increase children's ability to self-regulate as well as their ability to influence the environment. Gauvain's third topic is research focused on understanding the cultural contexts of cognitive development, particularly as it occurs in interactions with more experienced members of one's community. Thus her chapter offers a fitting ending to this volume, bringing together themes pertaining to biology, contexts, and culture that are addressed across all of the chapters included here.

Conclusion

To return to a quote that Goodnow cited in Chapter Nine, in the early eighteenth century Alexander Pope wrote, "'Tis education forms the common mind. Just as the twig is bent, the tree's inclined." Developmental scholars maintain elements of Pope's Enlightenment ideal. We still care deeply about providing nurturing and healthful environments for children and adolescents.

At the same time, we no longer see each child as a twig that we can bend in any direction, but rather as a person who comes into the world with emotional and cognitive tendencies that influence her or his developmental pathway. We no longer see an adolescent as a tree that early experiences have inclined in a fixed direction once and for all, but rather as an active, creative, and co-constructive member of society. Finally, we no longer see all persons as developing toward acquisition of one common mind, but rather as members of diverse cultures with varying educational and socialization goals.

References

National Research Council and Institute of Medicine (2002). *From neurons to neighborhoods: The science of early childhood development.* Washington, DC: National Academy Press.

Sharma, D. (Ed.) (2004). *Human technogenesis: Cultural pathways through the information age.* New Directions for Child and Adolescent Development, no. 105. San Francisco: Jossey-Bass.

LENE ARNETT JENSEN *is associate professor in the Department of Psychology at Clark University. Her research addresses the intersection of culture and development in moral reasoning, and immigrant identity development and civic engagement.*

REED W. LARSON *holds the Pampered Chef Endowed Chair in Family Resiliency in the Department of Human and Community Development at the University of Illinois, Urbana-Champaign. His current research focuses on youth programs as contexts of adolescent development.*

2

Over the past quarter century, the study of child and adolescent development has made important progress by using its theoretical insights to address the common problems of growing up. In light of findings generated by this empirical activity, it is now time to take a new look at the field's theoretical base to establish a comprehensive framework for understanding all the processes implicated in children's development, from the neural to the cultural.

Looking Back, for a Change: A Story of Directions in Child and Adolescent Development

William Damon

One of the first lessons in developmental theory that I learned as a graduate student (at a time when, as I note later, the field was paying exceptional attention to theory) was that chronological age neither defines nor causes development; rather, there is a direction to any developmental change that must be identified and examined if we are to fully understand that change. It was a lesson that helped me develop a habit of thinking about directionality—the question of where things might be headed and why—whenever I tried to study behavioral change. Of course, we never can know how or why something changes until we actually study it; but an eye for possible direction goes a long way toward building an interpretive framework for making sense out of the before-and-after comparisons that are at the heart of developmental data. A focus on directions can help us determine whether there is a logic, and if so what it is, to the changes that we observe.

A second theoretical lesson I remember from those years was that we can apply this kind of directional developmental analysis to virtually any set of phenomena, from the gestures of infants to the movement of planets. The history of an academic field, including the field of human development itself, may be included in this province. So it is my intention in this brief chapter to do just that, using as a database my own experience as prior editor of this child development series. My purpose in this "look backward" (a unique event for a series of volumes that have been dedicated exclusively to new directions) is to offer my personal view about where the field has been and where it might be heading in the future.

New Directions for Child and Adolescent Development, no. 109, Fall 2005 © Wiley Periodicals, Inc.

New Directions for Child and Adolescent Development was born during a time of intense theoretical debate. What appear now to be purely conceptual distinctions between contrasting approaches was infused with a philosophical and ideological import that sometimes raised the tenor of argumentation to a fevered pitch. Developmental theories were considered entire worldviews that determined everything from the judgments that people made to the values they lived by.

I founded the series in 1978. Ten years before, during the Paris student revolts of the Vietnam era, Howard Gardner made an astonishing observation: "The uprising of 1968 signaled a new shift in intellectual allegiance among the students. 'Structuralism is dead' cried the students. Whether or not they had ever read a word of Piaget or Levi-Strauss, they sensed a tie between the philosophy of these men and the establishment they had come to despise" (Gardner, 1972, p. 214).

Even in those days, to see scholarly theories protested in the streets was rare (although certainly noteworthy). The journals were another matter. Every assumption was fiercely contested, every theoretical debate had high-stakes meaning, and abstract academic rhetoric took on an air that sometimes veered toward the apocalyptic. For example, in 1974, just as I was finishing graduate school, I came across a cultural critique of the Kohlbergian moral development theory that I had studied as a student. This early statement of a cultural perspective, published in the touchstone journal *Human Development*, concluded in this manner:

> Perhaps our scientific search should be less for eternal verities and universal invariance than for alternative and creative modes of coping with the truly universal and eternal problems of justice and liberty. The moral reasoning which we see actively applied today by the Western world, quite apart from high-minded professional philosophy, bids fair to destroy man. We would do better to explore and analyze differences wherever found, to borrow and adapt, and to nurture invention and cultural mutation as it occurs, than to perpetuate the ideology of a suicidal world trying to reconcile its differences through the use of a theoretical framework ill-suited for containing and ordering real human diversity [Simpson, 1974, p. 103].

This indeed was taking psychological theory seriously. It would be hard today to find a scholarly conclusion that proposed a link between a particular theory of moral judgment and the fate of humankind, but at the time it almost seemed like a reasonable conjecture. The author was proposing that Kohlberg has implicitly devalued the moral perspectives of people living in non-Western cultures by claiming universality for a moral stage sequence founded on Western philosophical assumptions and empirically validated by research with Western subjects. This suggested the danger that such theoretical imperialism could lead to cultural conflict, and ultimately world destruction.

In some ways, such attention to the big picture was actually a welcome change for American psychology, which had just emerged from what was at last being dismissed as "dust-bowl empiricism." The field of child development, mercifully, moved past its long years of simply cataloguing skills and behaviors of children at various phases of their growth trajectories, or of recording "a day in the life of the child" from dawn to dusk (Wright, 1960). The broader theoretical debates of the 1960s and 1970s brought a new excitement and drama to the field and made a constructive mark on the kind of work that scholars were choosing to do.

The three "grand theories" that dominated the field at midcentury (behaviorism, cognitive-structuralism, and psychoanalysis) had wrestled with one another in the academic arena, with cognitive models gaining an upper hand. A the time, the main cognitive models were Piagetian, Vygotskian, and "information processing" (or what was soon to be called "cognitive science") theories, interspersed with some cultural lines of work descending from the Whitings' anthropological studies and some biological lines of work descending from animal ethology, behavior genetics, and the study of infant temperament. Textbooks of the era, in sharp contrast with those from prior decades, were organized around the concepts that had emerged from all this rich theoretical discussion. Ideas had become important in developmental science, and that was a good thing.

But by 1978, when I took on the task of envisioning "new directions" for this new journal, it did not seem to me that such theoretical discourse, however elevated, was sufficient to define the future of an enterprise as consequential as child development. Moreover, the highly charged extensions of psychological theory into the realm of social and political ideology seemed to me to be incommensurate with the goal of open-minded scientific inquiry. Nor, on the other hand, could a return to empty empiricism define future directions of any sort. What seemed apparent to me at the time was that the profound conceptual work that had gone into building and critiquing developmental theories could be better mined for its potential for helping us understand the common problems of growing up.

The developmental literature was full of fine, nuanced discussion contrasting universalism to contextualism; or comparing Piaget with Vygotsky; or making a case for nativistic, environmental, and interactional explanations of behavior; but it was hard to use the insights generated by these discussions to answer questions such as, How does television (and the then-new computer games) affect children's learning? What kind of friendship do youngsters benefit from? Why do so many youngsters gravitate toward antisocial and destructive behavior? Where do children find the goals and motives that influence their life choices? How do children experience parental divorce? What kind of variation in family patterns across time and social context shapes the perspectives of the young? Are today's children experiencing life differently from children of previous generations? These are questions of the kind that people outside our field seek answers to; and it occurred to me that insights from theoretically driven research in the field could answer the questions more directly than had been done in the past. I was by no means the only researcher at the time who made this observation, but as editor of a new journal I had choices to make that extended beyond my own research program. I decided to go with topics representing problems of general interest that could be addressed by state-of-the-art theory and data. At the same time, I was sure that grappling with such problems would inform our theory building, so that the benefits of such an enterprise would flow two ways, from theory to problem and back again.

It was easy enough to find authors and volume editors, since there were plenty of talented people doing such work. But their work was usually confined to standard journal articles, stripped down without much conceptual context, or in the occasional monograph that was usually isolated from fieldwide trends. What was missing was a regular outlet for such work that allowed authors to communicate their full intentions and achievements to readers in the field.

My purposes for the series, then, were to (1) offer an outlet for theoretically driven, innovative research that addressed recognized problems in the field; (2) publish the writings quickly, so they could have an immediate impact on other researchers, in particular students and young scholars who would use the journal as a source for their own ideas; (3) give authors a chance to develop their full argument as well as the rationale behind their approach; and (4) forge connections between researchers who were after the same goals, so they would build on one another's work. In this way, I hoped that we might make progress in the study of important problems while advancing the interests and directions of the field at large.

Without singling out particular topics from the hundred-plus volumes that we have put together since 1978 (any attempt to do so would seem arbitrary at best), it is fair to say that work first published in this series anticipated much of the progress made by the field during this period. The field has made enormous progress in its efforts to explore the central problems and processes of child and adolescent development. In another role that I took on during these years, as editor of the two most recent editions (1998 and 2006) of the encyclopedic *Handbook of Child Psychology* I have been amazed at how rapidly the field expanded its knowledge base since the 1970 edition of the *Handbook* that I pored over as a student. We now have a deeper, more complex, and more useful understanding about virtually every topic in the field than we did at that time, a few years before this series was founded.

Which brings me back to the question of directions in the development of our developmental field. As I have indicated, since the middle of the previous century there has been a rotation from empiricism to theory building to problem-based research (an empirical enterprise of a different sort) on the field's center stage. This movement has yielded much fruit, as the *Handbook* or any of the latest textbooks will show.

But progress itself always poses new challenges for any field. In our field, some great advances—for example, in examining the neural bases of cognition and behavior—have taken us in dramatically different directions than other advances have—for example, in examining the cultural bases of cognition and behavior. At some point, these and other advances must be integrated with one another if we are still to have one field rather than many. For this to occur, new and better theories must be constructed. So we may be ready to return to another era of heightened attention to theory building, now supplied by the revealing findings of the past quarter century and driven this time by the scientific goals of discovery.

References

Gardner, H. (1972). *The quest for mind.* New York: Random House.

Simpson, E. L. (1974). Moral development research: A case study of scientific bias. *Human Development, 17,* 81–106.

Wright, H. (1960). Observational child study. In P. Mussen (Ed.), *Handbook of research methods in child development.* New York: Wiley.

WILLIAM DAMON is professor of education and director of the Center on Adolescence at Stanford University. Damon has written on moral development at all ages of human life. He is editor-in-chief of the Handbook of Child Psychology *(fifth and sixth editions).*

PART TWO

Self-in-Culture

3

Demographic shifts in the U.S. population require developmental researchers to increase their attention to cultural diversity. Conceptual models that incorporate culturally relevant variables and focus on normative and positive development are needed to produce a more balanced understanding of Latino youth development.

Understanding Latino Children and Adolescents in the Mainstream: Placing Culture at the Center of Developmental Models

Marcela Raffaelli, Gustavo Carlo, Miguel A. Carranza, Gloria E. Gonzalez-Kruger

The presence of Spanish-speaking people and their descendents in what are now parts of the United States of America dates back to the early sixteenth century. Despite this presence, Latino families and their children have been inadequately—and sometimes inaccurately—represented in the developmental literature. (In this chapter, the term *Latino* is used to refer to both male and female persons of Mexican, Puerto Rican, Cuban, and Central or South American origin or descent, regardless of race; Day, 1996.) It is our belief that to remedy this situation developmental scholars must do three things. First, explicit attention must be paid to cultural diversity between and within subgroups of Latino youth. Second, there is a need for research on normative and positive development in this population. Third, developmental models must meaningfully incorporate culturally relevant factors. In this essay, we elaborate on each of these suggestions and describe an integrated model we are using to guide our work on Latino youth development.

The authors are grateful for input from their colleagues in the Latino Research Initiative (LRI) and acknowledge the institutional support the LRI has received over the years. Manuscript preparation was partially supported by a Faculty Development Fellowship to Marcela Raffaelli from the College of Arts and Sciences, University of Nebraska-Lincoln, and by a Visiting Fellowship at the Key Centre for Women's Health in Society, School of Population Health, University of Melbourne.

Diversity of the Latino Population: Historical and Demographic Considerations

Historical and demographic considerations point to variations between Latino youths and those from other ethnic groups, as well as among Latino subgroups, that have important implications for developmental research.

Colonization, Conquest, and Migration: A Brief History. The U.S. Latino population consists of Latino groups with varied histories, including long-term residents and more recent immigrants. For several centuries, territory that is now part of the United States was populated by indigenous peoples, Spanish colonists, and Mexican citizens. At one time, Spanish territories encompassed what are now the states of New Mexico, Texas, California, and Florida, as well as Puerto Rico and other Caribbean islands. During the eighteenth and nineteenth centuries, as wars were fought, treaties negotiated, and borders redrawn, Spanish Americans (primarily Mexicans) became an integral part of the United States. More recently, Latin American immigrants have followed a number of pathways to the United States. Since gaining independence, the United States has sought to influence events in Latin America through policy, diplomacy, and active intervention. The impact of these policies within Latin America is widespread; they also shape the experiences of Latinos in the United States. For example, during the second half of the twentieth century, citizens of some Latin American countries (an example is Cuba) were granted refugee status and resettlement assistance on entering the United States. In other countries (such as El Salvador), the United States supported repressive dictatorships, spurring a flow of often undocumented immigrants fleeing political violence and terror. Lack of economic opportunities in other nations (for instance, Mexico) led to a flow of migrant workers and undocumented immigrants that continues to this day. The diverse history of the Latino population in the United States would be expected to influence Latino youth development.

Demographic Characteristics of Latino Youth. According to the 2000 U.S. Census, Latino children and adolescents now represent 17 percent of the under-eighteen population (Lugalla & Overturf, 2004), and it is projected that this proportion will increase to one-third by the year 2050 (U.S. Department of Health and Human Services, 2001). As shown in Table 3.1, Latino youths differ from those of other ethnic groups in ways that are likely to affect socialization and life experiences, ultimately influencing their development and well-being. For example, Latino youths are more likely to be foreign-born than white and black youths, more likely than white and Asian youths to live in poverty, and more likely than all other youths to have at least one parent who is not a high school graduate.

There are also significant variations between Latino subgroups that it is essential to consider (Baca Zinn, 1995; Gouveia, Carranza, & Cogua, in press). Among them are geographic concentration patterns (for example, most Cuban Americans live in the South, whereas Mexican Americans

Table 3.1. Key Chaacteristics of Latino and Non-Latino Children Under Eighteen Years Old

	Hispanic or Latino[a] 12,148,066	White 49,282,114	Black 10,594,324	Asian 2,423,951
Number				
Foreign-born, %	14.1	2.5	2.0	26.7
Speak only English at home, %	21.1	65.3	69.5	22.4
Live with married parents, %	62.6	76.0	34.6	82.7
Family below poverty line, %	26.5	10.5	31.8	13.6
Multigenerational household, %	15.6	6.7	16.8	17.8
At least one parent not high school graduate, %	51.9	17.1	23.3	25.1
At least one parent recent immigrant (past five years), %	8.7	1.9	1.4	15.7
At least one parent foreign-born, %	55.7	11.1	8.8	86.5

Notes: Figures do not include individuals of two or more races.

[a]Hispanics or Latinos can be of any race.

Source: U.S. Census Bureau (2000).

are concentrated in the West), demographic characteristics (educational achievement, socioeconomic status), and immigration-related factors (generation of immigration, home language). Foreign-born Latinos vary in preimmigration experience (reason for departure), postimmigration experience (availability of ethnic enclaves), and individual characteristics (age on arrival and others).

These variations between Latino youths and those from other ethnic groups, as well as among Latino subgroups, have implications for children's and adolescents' development—and thus for developmental research.

Implications for Developmental Research. Despite the heterogeneity of the U.S. youth population as revealed in Table 3.1, researchers conducting general developmental studies have seldom collected the kind of information needed to examine within-group differences, Latinos included. However, to better understand development it is imperative that research studies take within-group variations into account. In the case of Latinos, it would be desirable to assess such basic indicators as Latino subgroup, generation of immigration, language used at home, and parental education and income (see also Umaña-Taylor & Fine, 2001). This information can be used to describe the sample and if necessary control for subgroup differences in statistical analyses. Researchers should also temper their conclusions and avoid making unwarranted generalizations that assume Latinos form one amorphous group. These minor yet critical changes represent an important first step in broadening the knowledge base on Latino youth development.

Studying Normative Development of Latino Youth

A second step in improving our understanding of Latino youth involves overcoming a historical tendency to take a comparative and deficit perspective in research with Latinos (and other ethnically diverse populations; see for example Fisher et al., 2002; MacPhee, Kreutzer, & Fritz, 1994). The comparative perspective typically defines European Americans as the norm and considers how other ethnic groups differ from that norm (Gonzalez-Kruger, Umaña-Taylor, Goldfarb, & Villarruel, 2003). In consequence, within-group variations are ignored; moreover, deviations from the European American pattern are often interpreted as indicating inferiority rather than potentially legitimate differences in functioning (Fisher et al., 2002). As well, developmental research has been disproportionately focused on problems within Latino communities (such as teen pregnancy, school dropout rate; see García Coll et al., 1996; MacPhee et al., 1994). The net result is a lack of basic information about normative developmental experiences of Latino youth (McLoyd, Cauce, Takeuchi, & Wilson, 2000; Parke & Buriel, 1998; Rodriguez & Morrobel, 2002).

There are encouraging signs that developmental scholars have seriously considered these concerns about research with ethnically diverse populations.

For example, a recent analysis of articles published in the *Journal of Research on Adolescence* between 1999 and 2003 indicated that almost half of the articles had ethnically diverse samples (although only 8 percent of articles focused primarily on Latinos), fewer than 10 percent of all articles compared ethnic groups, and articles focusing on European Americans were more likely to be problem-focused than those involving ethnically diverse youth (Larson & Cauce, 2004). There has also been a recent surge in research on normative development of Latino youths (and those of other ethnic groups; Fisher, Jackson, & Villarruel, 1998; McLoyd & Steinberg, 1998; Montero-Sieberth & Villarruel, 2000). This recent scholarship represents an important step; however, it has also revealed the conceptual and empirical challenges researchers face when trying to take culture seriously in developmental research. We turn next to an examination of these issues.

Representing Culture in Developmental Models

Research on Latino youth has drawn primarily on two approaches for considering culture in the study of development. The first involves attempting to incorporate culture into existing models, and the second places culture at the center of the model. Each approach offers advantages and disadvantages and requires explicit decisions to be made regarding how to represent cultural variables.

Incorporating Culture into Existing Developmental Models. Attempts to develop universal models of development, or to examine common developmental experiences, are important sources of knowledge. However, efforts to develop comprehensive developmental theories that integrate cultural variables are rare (Rogoff, 2003). Moreover, even when theorists incorporate culture into their models, researchers often fail to operationalize cultural variables adequately (McLoyd, 2004). For example, to permit incorporation of multiple ethnic groups, proxy variables such as education or birthplace or higher-order constructs such as individualism-collectivism are often used in lieu of culturally specific factors and values. In addition, mainstream developmental models often omit or relegate to the periphery factors highly salient to ethnic minority youth, such as experiences of racism (discrimination, prejudice) and social stratification (segregation; García Coll et al., 1996). Among Latino youth, issues of language and immigration are often particularly salient. Recently, in recognition of the difficulty of representing these factors within existing developmental models, scholars have begun to generate culture-specific models of development—a "paradigm shift" (García Coll & Magnusson, 1999) that we believe can lead to a fuller understanding of Latino youth development.

Placing Culture at the Center. A number of scholars have developed models that allow them to examine specific developmental experiences among multiple ethnic groups, including Latinos. For example, Jean Phinney's program of research on ethnic identity builds on and extends traditional work on ego identity by examining how youngsters from various ethnic backgrounds come to grips with the role of ethnicity in their lives (Phinney, Cantu, & Kurtz, 1997). The work of Carola and Marcelo Suárez-Orozco (2001) explores how individual and family functioning is affected by the experience of immigration. Catherine Cooper's program of research (1999) integrates culture into developmental perspectives on individuality and connectedness. This work underscores the value of developing models that explicate the role of culture in development.

Others have addressed the need for comprehensive developmental models that accurately reflect ethnically diverse youngsters' lives. For example, García Coll and colleagues (1996) generated a comprehensive model for studying the development of children of color. Racism and social stratification variables are central to the model, reflecting the pervasive influence of these variables on children's immediate environments and developmental experiences. Our research team has been pursuing a multidisciplinary program of community-based research in the Midwest (Gonzalez-Kruger et al., 2000). We are articulating an integrated model for examining the development of Latino children and adolescents growing up in immigrant families. The model, depicted in Figure 3.1, draws on three theoretical frameworks: Laosa's model (1990) of the development of immigrant Latino children, Berry's model of the role of acculturative stress in Latino youth adjustment (Berry, Kim, Minde, & Mok, 1987), and Lazarus and Folkman's model of stress and coping (1984).

Consistent with mainstream developmental models, we included a set of variables thought to influence children's cognitive and emotional development: characteristics of youngsters, their families and peer groups, and their everyday settings. Unlike traditional models, however, this model incorporates culturally relevant factors previously identified as important for Latino youth. For example, community and school context variables include the proportion of Latinos in the community or type of bilingual education program in school. Family, child, and peer characteristics encompass national origin, family form (transnational, binational, extended), age of child on arrival in the United States, and cultural background of peers. Cognitive and emotional factors include appraisals, identified in general models of stress and coping (Compas, 1987), and ethnic identity, an aspect of identity that is particularly salient for ethnically diverse youth (Phinney et al., 1997).

In addition, the model incorporates acculturative stress as an important intervening factor between antecedent and outcome variables. Acculturation is the process of adaptation that occurs when two cultural groups come into contact (Marín & Marín, 1991); acculturative stress refers to physiological and psychological changes brought about by acculturation-related demands (Berry et al., 1987). The centrality of acculturative stress in our model reflects research findings that adaptation of Latino families to the dominant culture is associated with family conflict and individual stress perceptions (Gil & Vega, 1996). Finally, the model explicitly recognizes

Figure 3.1. Theoretical Model of Latino Youth Development

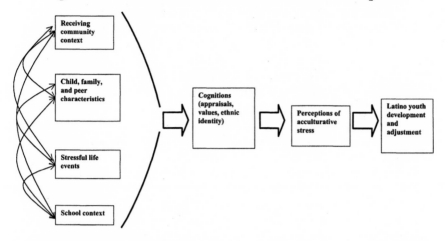

that although Latinos experience adversity they also have strengths and resources. For example, they can draw on cultural belief systems that help them deal effectively with life challenges, among them values supporting family connectedness and respect for authority and elders. These cultural values and practices foster ethnic identity (Phinney et al., 1997) and collaborative behavior (Knight, Bernal, & Carlo, 1995).

Although we have not yet tested the entire model within a single study, recent work by members of our team demonstrates the value of placing culture at the core of developmental research. For example, culturally relevant variables have emerged as important predictors of socialization practices in Latino families. In one set of analyses, parental national origin (Mexican versus other Latino origin) was linked to extent of communication about sexuality (Raffaelli & Green, 2003); in another, acculturation and parental preference for same-ethnicity romantic partners were related with ethnic identity achievement among nineteen- to thirty-year-old Latino college students (Ontai-Grzebik & Raffaelli, 2004). In an examination of linkages between characteristics of parent and peer relationships and behavioral outcomes, de Guzman and Carlo (2004) reported that Latino youths who reported secure attachment with peers and highly adaptable family systems exhibited a high level of prosocial behaviors. These findings highlight the potential of our integrated model for creating a framework for studying Latino youth development.

Concluding Thoughts

It is our belief that developmental research aimed at understanding Latino children and adolescents must take an explicit cultural focus. In this chapter, we have argued that scholars must attend not only to between-group differences but also to within-group diversity, examine normative developmental experiences, and develop models that meaningfully incorporate culturally relevant factors. Considerable progress toward these goals has been made in recent years. In particular, scholars have addressed many of the conceptual, ethical, and methodological issues involved in studying ethnically diverse youth, and guidelines for conducting culturally competent studies have been published (Marín & Marín, 1991). This literature is a solid basis on which to build in the future.

We hope that we have adequately conveyed the extent to which this literature is relevant not only for researchers who study Latinos but also for those who focus on mainstream populations. The U.S. population is undergoing its most dramatic transformation since the early nineteenth century. According to census projections, by the year 2050 just half the U.S. population will be "non-Hispanic White," down from three-quarters in 1990 (Day, 1996). Currently, one fifth of U.S. residents are either foreign-born or children of foreign-born parents, and this number will continue to grow. Thus, within the next twenty-five years all developmental research will either explicitly or implicitly involve the study of culturally and ethnically diverse youth. Failure to take these demographic realities into account will lessen the relevance of *all* developmental research.

References

Baca Zinn, M. (1995). Social science theorizing for Latino families in the age of diversity. In R. E. Zambrana (Ed.), *Understanding Latino families: Scholarship, policy, and practice* (pp. 177–189). Thousand Oaks, CA: Sage.

Berry, J. W., Kim, U., Minde, T., & Mok, D. (1987). Comparative studies of acculturative stress. *International Migration Review, 31*, 491–511.

Compas, B. E. (1987). Coping with stress during childhood and adolescence. *Psychological Bulletin, 101*, 393–403.

Cooper, C. R. (1999). Multiple selves, multiple worlds: Cultural perspectives on individuality and connectedness in adolescent development. In A. S. Masten (Ed.), *The Minnesota symposia on child psychology,* vol. 29: *Cultural processes in child development* (pp. 25–27). Hillsdale, NJ: Erlbaum.

Day, J. C. (1996). *Population projections of the United States by age, sex, race, and hispanic origin: 1995 to 2050.* (Current Population Reports, P25–1130.) Washington, DC: U.S. Census Bureau.

de Guzman, M.R.T., & Carlo, G. (2004). Family, peer, and acculturative correlates of prosocial development among Latinos. *Great Plains Research, 14,* 185–202.

Fisher, C. B., Jackson, J. F., & Villarruel, F. A. (1998). The study of African American and Latin American children and youth. In W. Damon (Series Ed.) & R. M. Lerner (Vol. Ed.), *Handbook of child psychology,* vol. 1: *Theoretical models of human development* (pp. 1145–1207). New York: Wiley.

Fisher, C. B., Hoagwood, K., Boyce, C., Duster, T., Frank, D. A., Grisso, T., Levine, R. J., Macklin, R., Spencer, M. B., Takanishi, R., Trimble, J. E., & Zayas, L. H. (2002). Research ethics for mental health science involving ethnic minority children and youths. *American Psychologist, 57,* 1024–1040.

García Coll, C., Lamberty, G., Jenkins, R., Pipes McAdoo, H. P., Crnic, K., Wasik, B. H., & Garcia, H. V. (1996). An integrative model for the study of developmental competencies in minority children. *Child Development, 67,* 1891–1914.

García Coll, C., & Magnusson, K. (1999). Cultural influences on child development: Are we ready for a paradigm shift? In A. S. Masten (Ed.), *The Minnesota symposia on child psychology, vol. 29: Cultural processes in child development* (pp. 1–24). Mahwah, NJ: Erlbaum.

Gil, A. G., & Vega, W. A. (1996). Two different worlds: Acculturation stress and adaptation among Cuban and Nicaraguan families. *Journal of Social and Personal Relationships, 13*(3), 435–456.

Gonzalez-Kruger, G. E., Umaña-Taylor, A., Goldfarb, K., & Villarruel, F. A. (2003). What do we REALLY know about Latino families? A content analysis of refereed publications. Poster session at the National Council on Family Relations (NCFR) Conference, Vancouver, British Columbia, Nov.

Gonzalez-Kruger, G., Zamboanga, B., Carlo, G., Raffaelli, M., Carranza, M. A., Hansen, D., Cantarero, R., & Gajardo, J. (2000). The Latino research initiative: A multidisciplinary and collaborative community-university outreach and scholarship model. *Great Plains Research, 10,* 359–385.

Gouveia, L., Carranza, M. A., & Cogua, J. (in press). The Great Plains migration: Mexicanos and Latinos in Nebraska. In V. Zuniga & R. Hernandez-Leon (Eds.), *New destinations of Mexican immigration in the United States: Community formation, local responses, and inter-group relations.* New York: Sage.

Knight, G. P., Bernal, M. E., & Carlo, G. (1995). Socialization and the development of cooperative, competitive, and individualistic behaviors among Mexican American children. In E. E. García & B. McLaughlin (Eds.), *Meeting the challenge of linguistic and cultural diversity in early childhood education* (pp. 85–102). New York: Teachers College Press.

Laosa, L. (1990). Psychosocial stress, coping, and development of Hispanic immigrant children. In F. C. Serafica & A. I. Schwebel (Eds.), *Mental health of ethnic minorities* (pp. 38–65). New York: Praeger.

Larson, R., & Cauce, A. M. (n.d.). SRA and diversity: The results of a membership survey. Available at http://s-r-a.org/SRA.diver.report.htm. Retrieved Dec. 5, 2004.

Lazarus, R. S., & Folkman, S. (1984). *Stress, appraisal and coping.* New York: Springer.

Lugalla, T., & Overturf, J. (2004). *Children and the households they live in: 2000.* (Census 2000 Special Reports, CENSR-14.) Washington, DC: U.S. Census Bureau.

MacPhee, D., Kreutzer, J. C., & Fritz, J. J. Infusing a diversity perspective into human development courses. *Child Development,* 1994, *65,* 699–715.

Marín, G., & Marín, B. V. (1991). *Research with Hispanic populations.* Thousand Oaks, CA: Sage.

McLoyd, V. C. (2004). Linking race and ethnicity to culture: Steps along the road from inference to hypothesis testing. *Human Development, 47,* 185–191.

McLoyd, V. C., Cauce, A. M., Takeuchi, D., & Wilson, L. (2000). Marital processes and parental socialization in families of color: A decade review of research. *Journal of Marriage and the Family, 62,* 1070–1093.

McLoyd, V., & Steinberg, L. (1998). *Research on minority adolescents: Conceptual, methodological, and theoretical issues.* Hillsdale, NJ: Erlbaum.

Montero-Sieberth, M., & Villarruel, F. A. (Eds.) (2000). *Making invisible Latino adolescents visible.* New York: Falmer Press.

Ontai-Grzebik, L. L., & Raffaelli, M. (2004). Individual and social influences on ethnic identity among Latino young adults. *Journal of Adolescent Research, 19,* 559–575.

Parke, R. D., & Buriel, R. (1998). Socialization in the family: Ethnic and ecological perspectives. In N. Eisenberg (Ed.), *Handbook of child psychology, vol. 3, Social, emotional, and personality development* (5th ed.) (pp. 463–552). New York: Wiley.

Phinney, J., Cantu, C. L., & Kurtz, D. A. (1997). Ethnic and American identity as predictors of self-esteem among African American, Latino, and white adolescents. *Journal of Youth and Adolescence, 26,* 165–185.

Raffaelli, M., & Green, S. (2003). Parent-adolescent communication about sex: Retrospective reports by Latino college students. *Journal of Marriage and Family, 65*, 474–481.

Rodriguez, M. C., & Morrobel, D. (2002). A review of Latino youth development research and a call for an asset orientation. *Hispanic Journal of Behavioral Sciences, 26*, 107–127.

Rogoff, B. (2003). *The cultural nature of human development.* New York: Oxford University Press.

Suárez-Orozco, C., & Suárez-Orozco, M. M. (2001). *Children of immigrants.* Cambridge, MA: Harvard University Press.

Umaña-Taylor, A., & Fine, M. A. (2001). Methodological implications of grouping Latino adolescents into one collective ethnic group. *Hispanic Journal of Behavioral Sciences, 23*, 347–362.

U.S. Census Bureau. (2000). Census 2000 PHC-T-30—characteristics of children under 18 years by age, for the United States, regions, states, and Puerto Rico: 2000. Available at http://www.census.gov/population/www/cen2000/phc-t30.html, tables 1 and 2. Retrieved Sept. 24, 2004.

U.S. Department of Health and Human Services. (2001). *Mental health: Culture, race, and ethnicity.* (Supplement to *Mental health: A report of the Surgeon General.*) Rockville, MD: U.S. Department of Health and Human Services.

MARCELA RAFFAELLI is professor of psychology and ethnic studies (Latino and Latin American studies) at the University of Nebraska-Lincoln.

GUSTAVO CARLO is professor of psychology at the University of Nebraska-Lincoln.

MIGUEL A. CARRANZA is associate professor of sociology and ethnic studies (Latino and Latin American studies) and director of the Institute for Ethnic Studies at the University of Nebraska-Lincoln.

GLORIA E. GONZALEZ-KRUGER is assistant professor in the Department of Family and Consumer Sciences and the Marriage and Family Therapy program at the University of Nebraska-Lincoln.

4

This chapter argues for the essential role of culture in forming the basic constructs and theories of developmental psychology. The case is made for the need to overcome the cultural insularity of core developmental concepts and methods in order to create a psychology that is more truly universal.

Essential Role of Culture in Developmental Psychology

Joan G. Miller

Posing an issue that persists over time in the field of psychology, Michael Cole introduced his recent volume on cultural psychology with a central puzzle: why "psychologists find it so difficult to keep culture in mind" (Cole, 1996, p. 1). As Cole observes: "On the one hand, it is generally agreed that the need and ability to live in the human medium of culture is one of the central characteristics of human beings. On the other hand, it is difficult for many academic psychologists to assign culture more than a secondary, often superficial role in the constitution of our mental life" (p. 1).

Psychologists routinely turn to culture for methodological control purposes, to confirm the universality of existing psychological theories or to identify factors that mediate or moderate particular psychological outcomes. Attention is paid to culture in these methodological and hypothesis testing senses, but culture tends to be given relatively little weight and to be viewed as nonessential in forming psychological constructs and theory.

Addressing this puzzle, this chapter explores the role of culture in understanding basic psychological processes. Through an overview of illustrative research in cultural psychology, the case is made that culture needs to be understood as critical to developmental psychology in a theory-construction sense, one that stands to enrich the field both conceptually and methodologically. In turn, the argument is forwarded that developing more sophisticated understandings of culture and overcoming the cultural insularity of core psychological constructs and methods constitute central challenges that must be met to succeed in identifying the constitutive role of culture in basic developmental processes and to create what is truly a more universal discipline.

NEW DIRECTIONS FOR CHILD AND ADOLESCENT DEVELOPMENT, no. 109, Fall 2005 © Wiley Periodicals, Inc.

Culture in Contemporary Developmental Psychology

With their sensitivity to contextual influences on behavior, developmental psychologists routinely attend to culture for methodological control as well as purposes of theory confirmation. In the former sense, for example, it is widely recognized that methodological bias may result if methodological procedures are not equivalent in meaning for individuals from differing age and cultural subgroups. It is this type of insight that has led researchers of cognitive development to emphasize the importance of using materials as well as response modes that are familiar to respondents; such insight has also made it possible to identify the presence of greater cognitive competences among various cultural populations than was once assumed, on the basis of their low scores on conventional intelligence test measures (Greenfield, 1997).

In terms of theory-confirmation purposes, culture is commonly taken into account in contemporary developmental psychology in testing the universality of existing theories. Most major developmental theories are routinely subject to cross-cultural testing to assess their presumed universality and identify processes that may account for variation in the rate of development or in the highest level of development obtained. Commonly such research either yields findings of universality or uncovers patterns in which middle-class European American participants are observed to develop more rapidly or obtain a higher level of developmental competence than participants from other sociocultural backgrounds—results that are explained in terms of variation in some underlying psychological processes. Thus, for example, the finding that more securely attached children are observed in middle-class European American communities than in other cultural and socioeconomic groups is seen as consonant with the universality of attachment processes (Ainsworth, Blehar, Waters, & Wall, 1978; Main, 1990). It is explained in terms of factors such as less socially responsive forms of parenting being emphasized in lower socioeconomic groups and various other sociocultural communities. Likewise, the finding that most cultural populations do not obtain the higher stage of postconventional moral development found among urban middle-class Western samples but instead reason purely at a conventional level is interpreted as congruent with the universality of Kohlbergian theory (Kohlberg, 1984; Nucci, 2002), while highlighting the importance of education and of experience in cognitively rich social environments in promoting the rate and highest level of moral development obtained.

This type of stance assumed in contemporary developmental psychology yields theories that appear to have impressive predictive power and explanatory force. Investigators point to consistency in the empirical links observed between psychological constructs across cultural settings as evidence for the construct validity as well as universality of theories. To illustrate, the external validity of self-determination theory (Deci & Ryan, 1985,

1990) is supported by findings that autonomy support shows the same empirical relationship to individual satisfaction and self-esteem within Bulgarian and U.S. samples (Deci and others, 2001).

Research in cultural psychology does not call into question the replicable nature of empirical findings of this type. Rather, its central challenge to such approaches is conceptual—that is, to point to overlooked cultural processes that contribute to such psychological effects and to uncover previously unrecognized modes of psychological functioning (Miller, 2004a). The concern is raised that to date major theories in developmental psychology tend to privilege middle-class European American outlooks and fail adequately to take into account contrasting cultural beliefs, values, and practices and their implications for basic psychological theory.

Developmental Research in Cultural Psychology

To illustrate the contributions of work in cultural psychology to developmental theory, a brief discussion is presented of examples of work in this tradition. The case is made that work in cultural psychology not only yields insights into the processes underlying developmental change but also contributes to a culturally broadened understanding of the endpoints and course of development.

Understanding of Self and Others. Cultural work on developing understanding of self and others has challenged the assumptions that the emergence of social knowledge can be explained fully in terms of self-constructive processes and that it proceeds along a universal developmental path. Early work in this area (Miller, 1984, 1986) demonstrated that the explanations individuals give for everyday social behaviors follow culturally variable developmental courses. Thus over the age range of eight to adolescence a significant developmental increase occurs among European American (although not among Hindu Indians) in the tendency to explain behaviors by reference to personality traits ("she is helpful"), but a significant developmental increase occurs over the same age range among Hindu Indians (although not among European Americans) in the tendency to explain behaviors by reference to contextual considerations ("she is his mother"). Such results suggest that developmental change results in part from processes of enculturation and cannot be fully explained in terms of cognitive and experiential factors.

More recently, this type of focus has been extended to the area of autobiographical memory and to self-understanding. Theoretically shifting the focus of work on infantile amnesia from the question of explaining why early autobiographical memories are lost to the question of what accounts for their formation, Nelson, Fivush, and their colleagues make the case that it is through participation in sociocultural "communities of minds" that autobiographical memories emerge (Fivush & Nelson, 2004; Nelson, 1993; Nelson et al., 2003). It is argued that through everyday discourse and social interaction children come to develop an understanding not only of a common past but of the significance of their particular outlook on the past. Further evidence that autobiographical memory depends on sociocultural processes is found in work showing that both the age of emergence of autobiographical memories and their content are culturally variable (Leichtman, Wang, & Pillemer, 2003; Wang, 2004).

In sum, cultural work on understanding of self and others contributes to developmental theory through revealing that developmental change reflects, in part, enculturation into culturally variable views of the self and cannot be fully explained by reference to the self-constructive processes emphasized in mainstream developmental psychology. Equally, it forwards new process accounts concerning the onset and nature of autobiographical memory.

Moral Development. Research in cultural psychology on moral development is yielding evidence for the need to broaden theoretical conceptions of the content of the moral domain, from the exclusive focus on issues of harm and justice associated with the Kohlbergian and distinct domain traditions (Kohlberg, 1984; Nucci, 2002; Turiel, 1998). Thus, for example, evidence suggests that the role-based considerations emphasized in many non-Western cultural communities represent an alternative form of postconventional morality that is not adequately represented within the Kohlbergian model (Snarey, 1985; Snarey & Keljo, 1991). Cultural work also reveals that the approach to the morality of caring articulated within Gilligan's morality-of-caring framework is culturally bound (Miller, 1994) with qualitatively distinct forms of the morality of caring emphasized within various cultural settings (Miller, 2001; Shimizu, 2001). In a critique of the exclusively secular focus of the dominant theoretical models of moral development, cultural work on morality also points to the need to recognize that spiritual concerns may be invested with moral force and are not invariably conceptualized as a matter of convention. Evidence is presented that in every culture morality encompasses not only issues of autonomy and community but also concerns with divinity (Jensen, 1998; Shweder, Much, Mahapatra, & Park, 1997).

In sum, cultural work demonstrates that the culturally variable views of self and others emphasized in cultural communities are linked to moral outlook. Highlighting the need to broaden existing theoretical understandings of morality, work on culture and moral development points to ways of making psychological models of morality less ethnocentric and more culturally inclusive.

Attachment. Processes of attachment constitute a fundamental aspect of human experience that is essential to survival in ensuring that the dependency needs of infants are met by their primary caregivers. The thrust of work in cultural psychology is not to challenge the importance or universal existence of attachment processes but rather to argue that the qualitative approach to attachment instantiated in contemporary attachment theory is culturally narrow and fails to take into account alternative cultural outlooks on attachment. As LeVine comments: "The metaphor of emotional security, so clearly a product of twentieth-century Euro-American notions of individual needs and interpersonal relations, is a remarkably recent and local concept on which to build a universal model of human development. . . . Neither the possibility that security of attachment was advantageous in human evolution nor its formal operationalization in reliable assessment procedures eliminates doubt about its status as a universal condition of mental health rather than a culturally contingent preference" (LeVine, 1989, p. x).

Reflecting this type of focus, cultural research documents that the concern with security emphasized within attachment theory more closely maps onto the beliefs and values emphasized within middle-class European American cultural communities than those emphasized within other cultural settings.

Cultural work on attachment conducted among Japanese populations, for example, calls attention to how concerns with empathy, interdependence, and indulgence of the other's needs that are related to the Japanese concept of *amae* do not fit closely with concerns with security that are emphasized in attachment theory (Rothbaum et al., 2000). The issue is not whether secure forms of attachment are broadly preferred to the insecure forms within Japan (which considerable evidence suggests they are; see, for instance, van IJzendoorn & Sagi, 2001). Rather, the concern is that, in emphasizing security, attachment theory in its present form does not fit closely with salient aspects of social behavior that are emphasized within Japanese cultural communities and reflected in their modes of parenting, such as emphasis on fitting in with others, loyalty, and interdependence. Parenting behaviors that embody these developmental goals, notably prolonged skin-to-skin contact with infants and responding in anticipation of rather than in response to the child's signals, constitute sensitive parenting within the Japanese context, though they are appraised as an indication of insecure attachment in terms of the assumptions of attachment theory.

To take another example, in attachment research that compared the outlooks of European American and Puerto Rican mothers, it was found that the former spontaneously emphasized concerns related to their child achieving a secure sense of self when asked both to describe their goals for their own child and to interpret the behavior of hypothetical children in the "strange situation" (Harwood, Miller, & Irizarry, 1995). In contrast, Puerto Rican mothers spontaneously brought up concerns related to maintaining a calm outlook and displaying respect and affection. The secure child was found to be a close match to the ideals that middle-class European American mothers held for their own children but did not capture the behavioral dimensions that Puerto Rican mothers considered of value, which were related to displaying proper demeanor and maintaining a contextually appropriate level of relatedness.

In sum, just as cultural work on moral development is pointing to constructs that are overlooked in theories of moral development, work on attachment in cultural psychology is likewise pointing to central dimensions of attachment in cultural communities that are not taken into account in how optimum attachment is defined. By expanding present conceptual models of attachment to capture more of the culturally variable constructs, goals, and practices that make up attachment processes in diverse cultural communities, work in this area is broadening the explanatory scope and cultural relevance of attachment theory.

Challenges and Contributions

The challenge for developmental psychology posed by research in cultural psychology is not only, or even necessarily primarily, to call into question the universality of existing psychological constructs and theories. Rather, its primary challenge is to the cultural inclusiveness and explanatory adequacy of these constructs and theories. In formulating conceptual models based on the beliefs, values, and practices emphasized in middle-class European American cultural communities, many major developmental theories are insufficiently sensitive to alternative, culturally variable modes of psychological functioning.

Overcoming this cultural insularity and achieving more culturally inclusive psychological theory requires greater sensitivity on the part of investigators. There is a need to go beyond the stereotypical formulations associated with the individualism-collectivism dichotomy and to base research on more nuanced understanding of cultural meanings and on greater attention to cultural practices (Miller, 2002; Kitayama, 2002). Equally, effort must be made to develop more culturally sensitive research methodologies (Miller, 2004b). In this regard, for example, it must be recognized that many of the standardized psychological scales so widely used in psychology are based on culturally narrow constructs and thus do not make it possible to tap culturally related psychological outlooks that do not map onto these constructs. Applying such research instruments allows us to identify apparent universals as well as uncover developmental trends in which certain populations do not obtain the higher level of development assumed in a theory; however, using such methodologies does not enable us to tap more culturally distinctive emphases that are not incorporated into the constructs tapped by the measures.

It must be recognized that cultural psychology does not eschew universals, deny the importance of biological influences on behavior, or assume that unique psychological theories must be formulated for every cultural community. Its goal is for cultural processes to be taken into account in psychology as a fundamental constitutive source of patterning of human development. Cultural psychology will achieve this goal when it ceases to exist as a distinct perspective within the discipline but, like explanatory approaches to psychology within biology, has become so fully integrated into psychology that a concern with culture is now implicated fundamentally in our constructs, methods, and basic theoretical explanatory models.

The gain from bringing culture more centrally into our basic constructs and theories is to capture the reality of human experience that is reflected in Cole's comment about culture as the ever-present medium of human development. Within contemporary developmental psychology, we tend to recognize cultural influences only fleetingly, as in the cross-cultural findings that are reported in our textbooks as an exception to an expected trend, or in multiyear life-span longitudinal studies that we recognize as having a somewhat dated quality that makes, for example, the experience of adolescents during the Depression appear less immediately relevant to that of present-day youth. However, the call of work from cultural psychology is to recognize that it is not merely the "other" and not merely our ancestors whose psychological functioning is affected by particular sociocultural historical experiences; this is a fundamental and inevitable aspect of all human experience. Psychology is always cultural, just as it is always biological; the recognition of this fact opens new theoretical insights and new areas of applied relevance.

The promise of taking culture into account more centrally in developmental psychology is to enable us to gain new conceptual insights into the nature of psychological processes that stand to enrich basic developmental theory. It will also enhance our effectiveness in applying developmental theory to social policy concerns, in making it possible for application of developmental theory to be more closely tailored to the outlooks and experience of individuals from diverse sociocultural backgrounds. This type of stance assumed in cultural psychology, it may be noted, is part of a broader effort to make psychology more inclusive of the perspectives of minority group populations and reduce the parochialism not only of its database but also of its core constructs and theories. By enriching our field, such efforts are essential in creating a discipline that recognizes the existence of culturally and subculturally variable successful pathways of human development, and thus that it is more truly universal.

References

Ainsworth, M. D., Blehar, M. C., Waters, E., & Wall, S. (1978). *Patterns of attachment: A psychological study of the strange situation.* Hillsdale, NJ: Erlbaum.

Cole, M. (1996). *Cultural psychology: A once and future discipline.* Cambridge, MA: Harvard University Press.

Deci, E. L., & Ryan, R. M. (1985). *Intrinsic motivation and self-determination in human behavior.* New York: Plenum.

Deci, E. I., & Ryan, R. M. (1990). A motivational approach to self: Integration in personality. In R. A. Dienstbier (Ed.), *Nebraska symposium on motivation: Perspectives on motivation,* vol. 38 (pp. 238–287). Lincoln: University of Nebraska Press.

Deci, E. L., Ryan, R. M., Gagne, M., Leone, D. R., Usunov, J., & Kornazheva, B. P. (2001). Need satisfaction, motivation, and well-being in the work organizations of a former Eastern Bloc country. *Personality and Social Psychology Bulletin, 27*(8), 930–942.

Fivush, R., & Nelson, K. (2004). Culture and language in the emergence of autobiographical memory. *Psychological Science, 15*(9), 573–577.

Greenfield, P. M. (1997). You can't take it with you: Why ability assessments don't cross cultures. *American Psychologist, 52,* 1115–1124.

Harwood, R. L., Miller, J. G., & Irizarry, N. L. (1995). *Culture and attachment: Perceptions of the child in context.* New York: Guilford Press.

Jensen, L. A. (1998). Moral divisions within countries between orthodoxy and progressivism: India and the United States. *Journal for the Scientific Study of Religion, 37*(1), 90–107.

Kitayama, S. (2002). Culture and basic psychological processes—toward a system view of culture: Comment on Oyserman et al. (2002). *Psychological Bulletin, 128*(1), 89–96.

Kohlberg, L. (1984). *The psychology of moral development: The nature and validity of moral stages.* San Francisco: Harper San Francisco.

Leichtman, M., Wang, Q., & Pillemer, D. P. (2003). Cultural variations in interdependence and autobiographical memory: Lessons from Korea, China, India, and the United States. In R. Fivush & C. A. Haden (Eds.), *Autobiographical memory and the construction of a narrative self: Developmental and cultural perspectives* (pp. 73–97). Mahwah, NJ: Erlbaum.

Main, M. (1990). Cross-cultural studies of attachment organization: Recent studies, changing methodologies, and the concept of conditional strategies. *Human Development, 33,* 48–61.

Miller, J. G. (1984). Culture and the development of everyday social explanation. *Journal of Personality and Social Psychology, 46*(5), 961–978.

Miller, J. (1986). Early cross-cultural commonalities in social explanation. *Developmental Psychology, 22,* 514–520.

Miller, J. G. (1994). Cultural diversity in the morality of caring: Individually oriented versus duty-based interpersonal moral codes. *Cross-Cultural Research: The Journal of Comparative Social Science, 28*(1), 3–39.

Miller, J. G. (2001). Culture and moral development. In D. Matsumoto (Ed.), *The handbook of culture and psychology.* New York: Oxford University Press.

Miller, J. G. (2002). Bringing culture to basic psychological theory: Beyond individualism and collectivism: Comment on Oyserman et al. (2002). *Psychological Bulletin, 128*(1), 97–109.

Miller, J. G. (2004a). The cultural deep structure of psychological theories of social development. In R. J. Sternberg & E. L. Grigorenko (Eds.), *Culture and competence: Contexts of life success* (pp. 11–138). Washington, DC: American Psychological Association.

Miller, J. G. (2004b). Culturally sensitive research questions and methods in social psychology. In C. Sansone, C. C. Morf, & A. T. Panter (Eds.), *The sage handbook of methods in social psychology* (pp. 93–116). Thousand Oaks, CA: Sage.

Nelson, K. (1993). The psychological and social origins of autobiographical memory. *Psychological Science, 4*(1), 7–14.

Nelson, K., Skwerer, D. P., Goldman, S., Henseler, S., Presler, N., & Walkenfeld, F. F. (2003). Entering a community of minds: An experiential approach to theory of minds. *Human Development, 46*(1), 24–46.

Nucci, L. P. (2002). The development of moral reasoning. In U. Goswami (Ed.), *Blackwell handbook of childhood cognitive development* (pp. 303–325). Malden, MA: Blackwell.

Rothbaum, F., Weisz, J., Pott, M., Miyake, K., & Morelli, G. (2000). Attachment and culture: Security in the United States and Japan. *American Psychologist, 55*(10), 1093–1104.

Shimizu, H. (2001). Japanese adolescent boys' senses of empathy (*omoiyari*) and Carol Gilligan's perspectives on the morality of care: A phenomenological approach. *Culture and Psychology, 7*(4), 453–475.

Shweder, R. A., Much, N. C., Mahapatra, M., & Park, L. (1997). The 'big three' of morality (autonomy, community, divinity) and the 'big three' explanations of suffering. In A. M. Brandt (Ed.), *Morality and health* (pp. 119–169). New York: Routledge.

Snarey, J. R. (1985). Cross-cultural universality of social-moral development: A critical review of Kohlbergian research. *Psychological Bulletin, 97*(2), 202–232.

Snarey, J. R., & Keljo, K. (1991). In a gemeinschaft voice: The cross-cultural expansion of moral development theory. In W. M. Kurtines & J. L. Gewirtz (Eds.), *Handbook of moral behavior and development: Theory,* vol. 1 (pp. 395–424). Hillsdale, NJ: Erlbaum.

Turiel, E. (1998). The development of morality. In N. Eisenberg (Ed.), *Handbook of child psychology: Social, emotional, and personality development,* vol. 3 (pp. 863–892). New York: Wiley.

Van IJzendoorn, M. H., & Sagi, A. (2001). Cultural blindness or selective inattention? *American Psychologist, 56*(10), 824–825.

Wang, Q. (2004). The emergence of cultural self-constructs: Autobiographical memory and self-description in European American and Chinese children. *Developmental Psychology, 40*(1), 3–15.

JOAN G. MILLER *is associate professor of psychology at the New School for Social Research in New York City.*

This chapter examines the development of self from the Hindu perspective, which views the Atman or inner self as the real self, transcending the empirical self that is socially embedded and subject to change across the life span and with intercultural contact.

5

Hindu Worldview in the Development of Selfways: The "Atman" as the Real Self

T. S. Saraswathi

The independent and interdependent self paradigm has received much attention in the field since the early nineties (see Greenfield & Cocking, 1994; Markus & Kitayama, 1994). More recently, the efficacy of this compelling paradigm is being questioned in terms of its explanatory power (Kitayama, 2002; Markus, Mullally, & Kitayama, 1997; Miller, 2002). Using the Hindu worldview, this chapter examines the possible existence of multiple combinations of the autonomous and the socially embedded selves, governed by sociohistorical as well as behavioral contexts and the specific stage in life-span development.

The principal arguments presented herein are that (1) to capture the complexity of the self seen as multifaceted, multivoiced, and multilevel, we need to move beyond the dichotomous classifications currently in vogue; (2) the Hindu worldview of the "Atman," or the spiritual self, considered as the real self, warrants examination; (3) both interindividual and intra-individual variations may be anticipated in the expression of selfways at the empirical level; (4) current literature focuses too little attention on developmental changes in construing the self across life stages; and (5) globalization and its consequences for the development of a multifaceted self must be taken into account.

NEW DIRECTIONS FOR CHILD AND ADOLESCENT DEVELOPMENT, no. 109, Fall 2005   © Wiley Periodicals, Inc.

Basic Issues and Concerns

The following section delineates the five basic issues just mentioned. In my opinion these form core concerns, though undoubtedly several more can be added in a detailed article on the topic.

Problematic Use of Dichotomous Classifications. Sinha and Tripathi (1994) present a critical argument regarding the use of dichotomies in psychological descriptions of individuals and cultures, stating that "such descriptive labels evoke unduly fixed and caricature-like mental impressions of cultures or societies rather than representative pictures of their complexities" (pp. 123–124).

In the Indian psyche, as well as in Indian modes of behavior, juxtaposition of opposites has been frequently observed and commented upon by travelers, writers, historians, and social scientists. There appears to be a high degree of tolerance for dissonance and coexistence of disparate elements without any felt need for synthesis either in individual behavior or in social practice. To quote Marriott (1976, cited in Sinha & Tripathi, 1994), "the seeming contradictions of thoughts and actions, instead of leading to confrontation, are tolerated, balanced, accommodated, and integrated" (p. 125). A telling example comes from A. K. Ramanujan, the world-renowned poet-philosopher who describes the ease with which his mathematician-astronomer father handled simultaneously his expertise in western science and Indian astrology, perceiving no contradictions in their coexistence (Ramanujan, 1990). Such juxtapositions of contradictory elements find emphasis in Indian philosophy and the traditional Indian medical system of Ayurveda, and even in today's daily lives of most educated Indians.

The caveat regarding "a perilous problem of cultural dichotomies," the common problem in psychology of investigating cultural differences as dichotomous distinctions, receives strong support in Hermans and his coauthors' theses related to dialogical processes in the development of self (Hermans and Kempen, 1998; Hermans, 2001), wherein self is viewed as multifaceted and multivoiced.

The Spiritual Self (Atman). Perhaps the most difficult concept of self to grasp cross-culturally is that posited in Hindu traditional thought (De Vos, Marsella, & Hsu, 1985). The concept of "real self" in Hindu thought is the Atman, a nonmaterial or metaphysical self, as opposed to the material, experiential forms of the empirical self involving sensations, desires, and thoughts. The empirical self is viewed as hierarchically lower than the metaphysical self. The Hindu Atman remains radically pervasive, the cynosure of Indian cognition and conation: "The empirical self, the ego as actor surrounded by other egos, is systematically marginalized in the Indian tradition so as to exalt the 'true,' i.e. the non-empirical self, often identified with the cosmic absolute pure and simple" (Bharati, 1985, p. 226). Undue importance given to the empirical self is considered Ahamkara (roughly translated as pride or arrogance), subjugation of which is essential for the realization of the real self or Atman. The perspective given here is not one of dichotomy between the empirical and the real self as much as transcendence of the latter moving beyond the former, empirical worldly self.

In fact, Bharati presents a radical argument that "it might just be possible that the Hindu self is indeed the philosophically most adequate intuition of selfhood, *if only it can be peeled out from beneath the recondite, arcane, obscurantist diction in which it has been encased*" (p. 227; emphasis added).

The Hindus are supposed to "know" that human action and decision making are prompted by karmic forces linked to a metaphysical notion of self, regardless of the extent of their knowledge of religious doctrines on Hindu philosophy. In fact, the Hindus feel that the true self can and should be realized, and the empirical self (mastery of which is seen as accounting for the consummate worldly success in the West) sublated. This process is seen as the consummation of human efforts, and success in the endeavor is expected to confer the most powerful charisma (as in the case of hermits and saints).

Consensual- and Individual-Level Cultures. At this juncture, I would like to clarify that my intention is not to claim that all Hindus work actively toward realization of the Atman (real self). However, it remains a guiding philosophy that permeates daily living, be it in toning down the individualistic pride (Ahamkara) while socializing a child or in accepting the calamities one confronts in life situations. Undoubtedly, there is a discrepancy between culture as perceived at the societal level and at the individual level wherein the individual actively constructs beliefs and practices on the basis of the contexts of life experience.

A related concern regards the view taken of culture as a monolith, implying that psychological phenomena take identical forms in all individualistic or collectivistic cultural populations or that basic psychological variation is of only two types (Miller, 2002). For example, even though both Japanese and Indians may be (in fact are) classified as interdependent, the inner boundary of the highly private inner self, a repository of individuality, varies greatly between the two groups. From his decades of psychoanalytic research work in Japan, India, and the United States, Roland posits that "the inner-most ego boundary varies even more between Indians and the Japanese, the former usually being far more in touch with their inner world than the latter and somewhat more so than North Americans" (1996, p. 19). The Hindu culture, though insisting on behavioral observation of proper social etiquette in family and group hierarchical relationships, gives considerable latitude to a variety of personal ideas, feelings, and fantasies. Hence a gap between public faces and private voices may be anticipated.

A Developmental Perspective. One major lacuna in the voluminous literature generated on the topic of the individualism-collectivism (see Kagitcibasi, 1997) and independent-interdependent construals of self (see Greenfield & Cocking, 1994) is the absence of focus on developmental changes. Reference is made to conscious socialization for independence in western cultures and for interdependence in a majority of the nonwestern cultures, but the assumption seems to be that following early socialization the two pathways become cultural end points. The Hindu worldview of the developing self challenges this viewpoint. A prescriptive religious philosophy deeply embedded in the psyche of the average Hindu (Bharati, 1985; Sinha & Tripathi, 1994), Hinduism delineates the acceptable code of conduct for each stage of life, recommending social embeddedness in the developmental stages until late middle age and disengagement and self-actualization in the last two life stages (Mistry & Saraswathi, 2003).

A brief note on Ashramadharma that describes the stages of the life cycle in the Hindu worldview may be pertinent at this juncture. These are the stages, as summarized succinctly by Ramanujan (1990) in terms of their sociocultural significance: *brahmacharya* ("celebrate studentship"), or preparation for a full relational life; *grhasthasrama* ("household stage"), full realization of it; *vanaprastha* ("the retiring forest-dweller stage"), loosening the bonds; and *sanyasa* ("renunciation" or "detachment"), cremation of all one's past and present relations.

Roland (1988) argues that the notion of detachment from immediate emotional connection, a theme central to Hindu spirituality, in some sense marks out the spiritual self as a realm of autonomy within the larger Hindu experience of unity. The call is to sublate the empirical self, once the major commitments of the householder's responsibilities are completed, and focus on realization of the true inner self or Atman, as that alone is real, the rest being illusion (or Maya). The call is to lead a life as water on the lotus leaf: on the leaf, yet aloof. This autonomy is acceptable and even expected.

Elaborating on this disengagement from early old age onward, Roland (1996) points out that detachment, a major factor in spiritual disciplines, may involve the pervasive, intense sensuality and sexuality of Indians. He argues that striving for brahmacharya, or sexual abstinence and renunciation in adulthood in the service of spiritual discipline, may also be viewed as a step in loosening the intense personal attachments and obligations in extended family-communal relationships and a reaching toward personal autonomy in the spiritual sphere. This is an argument most Indians would concur with (whether or not the belief translates to practice in their personal lives). The personal autonomy referred to here may be construed as a transcendental autonomy, an attempt to merge with the all-encompassing Atmans, in contrast to the autonomy of the empirical self that seeks separation and moving away from social interdependence.

With Indians, involvement with the spiritual is actually a mode of individuating and separating themselves from profound familial enmeshment, while still remaining connected with others (Roland, 1996). A pertinent example here would be women such as my aunts, who, even though enmeshed in the constant demands of running the household in a joint family setting, could create an inner space for themselves to withdraw into chanting the mantras, attending concurrently to cooking a meal or caring for an infant or two!

Conceptualizing individual autonomy in the hierarchical Indian society, Mines (1988), in his anthropological investigation, highlights evidence challenging the hierarchical, collectivist view of the Indian person: that as age increases, personal freedom and autonomy increase, making social embeddedness more a characteristic of the younger generation till middle age.

Analyzing twenty-three life histories of Indians, ranging in age from emerging young adulthood to old age, Mines draws the conclusion that there seem to be three stages of transition from interdependence to independence across the life span. The first stage is characterized by dependence on elders and conformity to cultural and social structural dictates. This is followed by a stage of early adulthood, where striving for autonomy is seen as rebellion. Later adulthood, however, is described by many of the respondents as striving for autonomy. Autonomy is defined as control over decision making affecting one's life, and a growing sense of responsibility for oneself.

Mines (1988) points out that as with all ideal model explanations, the hierarchical-collectivist view generates a distorted picture of the person and of motivation, because a person is depicted as passively trapped within the frame the model describes without any mechanism for generating change. What is evident in the histories studied by Mines is that aging propels the person through a series of stages in the social framework, each of which impinges on the individual in a particular way.

The emphasis in these arguments is on variability. As stated succinctly by Valsiner (2001), "variability—both intra-individual (over time) and inter-individual (across persons)—is the necessary part of phenomenological reality. It is precisely thanks to intra-individual variation over time that human development can occur at all" (p. 19).

Taking Change into Account. One criticism leveled against existing models of self-development is that they do not take developmental change into account. Another major source of change that has implications for individual adaptation is globalization and its consequences. Hermans and Kempen (1998) refer to it as the deterritorialization of culture.

Appadurai (1990), an Indian political anthropologist, describes five categories of global landscape that create new contact zones across national groups and cultures, leading to their deterritorialization in the modern world. They should be of particular interest to cross-cultural and developmental psychologists in understanding their influence on developmental pathways. The five categories of global landscapes, as described by Appadurai, are ethnoscapes (for example, immigrants, tourists, refugees, guest workers, exiles, and other moving groups); technoscapes (that is, global configuration of technology, both mechanical and informational); mediascapes (newspapers, television stations, film production studios); financescapes (currency markets, stock exchanges, commodity speculations); and ideoscapes (ideology of states and counterideologies of movements; ideas about freedom, rights, welfare).

In such a context, one cannot deal with culture as frozen in time or homogeneous. The caveat applies to such civilizations as China and India, which carry the tradition of five thousand or more years, as well as to more modern nation states in the West that "import" varied cultures via immigration. The implications of the changing global landscapes for the development of and changes in the independent and interdependent selfways need to be studied and understood.

In their essay in *American Psychologist,* with its captivating title "Moving Cultures: A Perilous Problem of Cultural Dichotomies in Globalizing Society," Hermans and Kempen (1998) focus on the accelerating process of globalization, the increasing interconnections between cultures, and the unprecedented challenge all of this poses to contemporary psychology. The challenge is particularly relevant to the approach of dichotomizing independent and interdependent selves and cultures.

The adaptive selves of immigrants and observations regarding bicultural identity serve as an illustrative example. The finding of particular interest is the joint existence of the independent and interdependent selves, especially among those who have adapted successfully in the host culture. Evidence indicates that among Indo-American second- and third-generation immigrants, the consensual or autonomous self assumes predominance depending on whether the behavior is in relation to the host culture or the home culture (J. Mistry, personal communication, 2004). Aktar (1995), a practicing Indian psychoanalyst on the West Coast of the United States, reviewing his twelve years of analytic experience with "native" and varied immigrant clients, including Indo-Americans, describes the emergence of a new and hybrid identity as a third individuation (the earlier two being the ones occurring in early childhood and then in adolescence).

Roland (2001) reiterates the point in arguing that globalization does not result in universalization but in interactive outcome, and consequently a range of psychological worlds. What is more, sociohistorical change is not necessarily the product of globalization and immigration alone but can emerge within cultures, as in the case of the feminist movement. The resulting hybridization is not a mere mix of X and Y but a new product altogether, depending on the cultural context and sociohistorical time. Anecdotal evidence based on reports from Indian expatriates suggests that although cultural heteronomy undoubtedly affects expression of the empirical self, the broad phases of the developmental stages of Ashramadharma are still evident, as is the search for the real self or Atman.

Concluding Comments: Alternative Approaches to the Study of Culture and Self

I loop back to the beginning wherein concern was expressed regarding the limitations of a dichotomous classification for understanding culture and self. The complex interweaving of self, culture, and development over the life course is further compounded by globalization and its consequences, resulting in the fast pace of change and the coexistence of alternative cultural demands (at times even contradictory in nature). This surely poses a challenge to cross-cultural developmental psychology. Several questions arise in our endeavor to unravel the complexity of a cultural self that is linked to all levels of self experience, developmental stages, and inner structures (including the Atman) as well as the experiences in a given sociohistorical era (Roland, 1996; Tripathi & Leviatan, 2003). The principal question from the Hindu worldview would be, Are the cultural changes referred to here reflected in the empirical self alone leaving the Atman or the real self unaffected? The answer is likely to be yes. Yet, the argument needs to be substantiated beyond mere "belief." At the same time, since it is the empirical self, whose functioning is witnessed as a dominant psychological phenomenon, the challenge to both theory and research is taking into account not only cross-cultural variability but also variability across situations or contexts, across life stages and sociohistorical time.

References

Aktar, S. (1995). A third individuation: Immigration, identity, and the psychoanalytic process. *Journal of the American Psychoanalytic Association, 43*(4), 1051–1084.

Appadurai, A. (1990). Disjuncture and differences in the global cultural economy. In M. Featherstone (Ed.), *Global culture: Nationalism, globalization, and modernity* (pp. 295–310). London: Sage.

Bharati, A. (1985). The self in Hindu thought and action. In A. J. Marsella, G. De Vos, & F.L.K. Hsu (Eds.), *Culture and self: Asian and western perspectives* (pp. 185–230). New York: Tavistock.

De Vos, G., Marsella, A. J., & Hsu, F.L.K. (Eds.) (1985). *Culture and self: Asian and western perspectives.* New York: Tavistock.

Greenfield, P. M., & Cocking, R. R. (Eds.) (1994). *Cross-cultural roots of minority child development.* Hillsdale, NJ: Erlbaum.

Hermans, H.J.M. (2001). The dialogical self: Toward a theory of personal and cultural positioning. *Culture and Psychology, 7,* 243–281.

Hermans, H.J.M., & Kempen, H.J.G. (1998). Moving cultures: A perilous problem of cultural dichotomies in globalizing society. *American Psychologist, 53*(10), 1111–1120.

Kagitcibasi, C. (1997). Individualism and collectivism. In J. W. Berry, M. H. Segall, & C. Kagitcibasi (Eds.), *Handbook of cross-cultural psychology,* vol. 3 (pp. 1–50). Boston: Allyn & Bacon.

Kitayama, S. (2002). Culture and basic psychological processes—toward a system view of culture: Comment on Oyserman et al. (2002). *Psychological Bulletin, 128*(1), 89–96.

Markus, H. R., & Kitayama, S. (1994). The collective fear of the collective: Implications for selves and theories of selves. *Personality and Social Psychology Bulletin, 20*(5), 568–579.

Markus, H. R., Mullally, P. R., & Kitayama, S. (1997). Self-ways: Diversity in modes of cultural participation. In U. Neisser and D. A. Jopling (Eds.), *The conceptual self in context: Culture, experience, self understanding* (pp. 13–61). Cambridge, UK: Cambridge University Press.

Miller, J. G. (2002). Bringing culture to basic psychological theory—beyond individualism and collectivism: Comment on Oyserman et al. (2002). *Psychological Bulletin, 128*(1), 97–109.

Mines, M. (1988). Conceptualizing the person: Hierarchical society and individual autonomy. *American Anthropologist, 90*(3), 568–579.

Mistry, J., & Saraswathi, T. S. (2003). The cultural context of child development. In I. Weiner (Series Ed.), *Handbook of psychology,* vol. 6: *Developmental psychology* (R. L. Lerner, A. Easterbrooks, & J. Mistry, Eds.) (pp. 267–291). New York: Wiley.

Ramanujan, A. K. (1990). Is there an Indian way of thinking? An informal essay. In M. K. Marriott (Ed.), *India through Hindu categories* (pp. 41–58). New Delhi: Sage.

Roland, A. (1988). *In search of self in India and Japan: Towards a cross-cultural psychology.* Princeton, NJ: Princeton University Press.

Roland, A. (1996). *Cultural pluralism and psychoanalysis: The Asian and North American experience.* New York: Routledge.

Roland, A. (2001). Another voice and position: Psychoanalysis across civilizations. *Culture and Psychology, 7*(3), 311–321.

Sinha, D., & Tripathi, R. C. (1994). Individualism in a collectivist culture: A case of coexistence of opposites. In U. Kim et al. (Eds.), *Individualism and collectivism: theory, method and applications,* vol. 16 (pp. 123–136). Cross-Cultural Research and Methodology series. Thousand Oaks, CA: Sage.

Tripathi, R. C., & Leviatan, U. (2003). Individualism and collectivism: In search of a product or process. *Culture and Psychology, 9*(1), 79–88.

Valsiner, J. (2001). Review essay. Contemplating self from India to contemporary self-psychology (review of Paranjpe [1998]). *Self and identity in modern psychology and Indian thought.* New York: Plenum). *Culture and Psychology, 7*(1), 115–118.

T. S. SARASWATHI is a cross-cultural developmental psychologist based in Bangalore, South India. She retired as senior professor in human development from the Maharaja Sayajirao University of Baroda, India.

6

*In this chapter, we argue that deeper insight into the
social nature of self-development can be gained by
adopting a dual focus on social relationships and meaning
making. A key challenge for future scholarship will be to
investigate the role of semiotic mediation in self-
construction during the early years of life.*

Developing Selves Are Meaning-Making Selves: Recouping the Social in Self-Development

Peggy J. Miller, Sarah C. Mangelsdorf

Most developmental theories share the assumption that self-development is
an inherently social process. The self develops in interaction with others;
even in cultures that celebrate individualistic selves no one develops a self
alone. The social nature of the self is central not only to theories of self-
development per se (Mead, 1934) but to theories of attachment (Bowlby,
1982), object relations (Mahler, Pine, & Bergman, 1975), and friendship
(Youniss, 1980) as well. Despite this consensus on so fundamental a point,
we still know little about self-construction as a social process. In this chapter, we identify three social arenas—(infant-caregiver relationships, early
conversations, and personal narrative)—that hold promise for illuminating
this process, focusing on the early years of life.

These social arenas are linked by another basic premise: that self-
construction is a meaning-making process. The self emerges in the crucible
of social relations, but those relations are embedded in cultural contexts and
mediated by language and other semiotic systems. Long before they are able
to comprehend words, babies derive meaning from touch, intonation, and
gaze, building practical understanding of self and parent. Once language
emerges, another kind of self-understanding becomes possible. According to
G. H. Mead (1934), self-formation depends on the ability to be an object
to oneself, a reflexive achievement made possible only through language.
Recent attempts to extend Vygotskian theory highlight the role of discourse-
level language, especially narrative, in creating self and identity (Miller, 1994;

NEW DIRECTIONS FOR CHILD AND ADOLESCENT DEVELOPMENT, no. 109, Fall 2005 © Wiley Periodicals, Inc.

Holland, Lachicotte, Skinner, & Cain, 1998). Thus, here again, theoretical traditions converge on an idea that is not new but whose potential has not been sufficiently realized in empirical work.

In this chapter, we argue that deeper insight into the social nature of self-development can be gained by maintaining a dual focus on social relationships and communicative mediation. Self-construction is a dynamic process that is affective, social, cognitive, cultural, and communicative; it is structured simultaneously at multiple levels (individual, family, culture). We identify a number of questions for future research, paying particular attention to questions that focus on the semiotic mediation of experience. We suggest that a key challenge for future scholarship is to investigate the role of semiotic mediation in self-construction, including changes from nonverbal to verbal to narrative mediation during the early years of life. We conclude by arguing that a focus on semiotic mediation also leads to fresh insights into the cultural construction of selves.

Infant-Caregiver Relationships: Origins of Self-Understanding

The first steps toward self-understanding are a by-product of the infant's developing relationship with caregivers. Early self-understandings are inherently affective, and mediated by nonverbal systems of meaning (Bretherton, 1991; Sroufe, 1990). According to Bowlby (1982), infants come into the world prepared to engage in social relations—to gaze at human faces, attend to human voices, respond to touch—and as a result of ongoing interaction develop internal representations or "working models" of attachment figures and of themselves.

However, we still know relatively little about how these critically important models get created. Valuable hints are found in fine-grained analysis of early infant-caregiver interaction (for example, Stern, 1985; Tronick, 1989). Stern (1985) observed that middle-class American infants and their caregivers establish synchronized routines, or "dances," within the first few months of life. His frame-by-frame analyses documented how both mother and infant initiate (baby uses arm and leg movements, social smiles, vocalization) and terminate (baby uses gaze aversion) interactions. Stern suggests that affective experiences in the first six months of life are one of the "invariants" of the developing self.

We accept Stern's point about affective experience but note that in some cultures caregiver-infant interactions privilege certain channels of communication, favoring body contact and disfavoring vocalization and direct gaze (LeVine, 1989). Thus one important question that bridges attachment research and cross-cultural research on communication concerns the kind of caregiver-infant dances that occur normatively in various groups. What do these dances look like? Which nonverbal channels are employed? What are the implications of these differences for very early self-development?

Stern's work is consistent with attachment theorists' claim that infants' working models involve expectations about how attachment figures will respond to events. Infants develop reciprocal models of self and other (my parent is loving; I'm lovable). According to attachment theory, this early sense of self is essentially evaluative, involving implicit, nonverbal understanding. Emde (1983) has called this sense of self "pre-representational," in that it exists before children have the ability for abstract mental representation. Are these models less susceptible to change *because* they are nonverbal? What happens to these nonverbal models once children are able to communicate verbally? The latter is a fundamental question not only for attachment researchers but also for Vygotskian theory, which assumes that a child's mastery of a new semiotic system results in a qualitative reorganization of meaning making.

A related point concerns the global evaluative nature of early working models. According to attachment researchers, children develop a conception of themselves as good or bad, depending on their attachment relationship; this claim is supported by Cassidy (1988). The notion of internal working models may therefore be helpful for understanding the acquisition of global self-concepts (such as self-esteem) and most certainly would aid in apprehending typical versus atypical self-concept development (Bretherton, 1991). However, it is not helpful for predicting the rather substantial variability evidenced in normal children's self-concept by age three years (Eder & Mangelsdorf, 1997). How then might children develop these more differentiated conceptions of their world and their place in it? We suggest that it is through conversation with parents and other family members that children begin to internalize a more differentiated view of themselves.

Early Conversations About Emotion: Building More Complex Self-Understanding

Although there is much literature on the socialization of emotion (see Denham & Kochanoff, 2002; Harris, 1989; and Saarni, 1999 for reviews), there have been fewer attempts to explore how emotion socialization may be related to children's self concept (Eder & Mangelsdorf, 1997; Thompson, 1998). Eder and Mangelsdorf speculated about the influence of early temperament on the developing self-concept. In their view, temperament consists of individual differences in expression of basic emotions such as fear, anger, and happiness (Campos et al., 1983). For example, some children have a lower threshold for responding to stressful events with fear than others. Such differences surely must result in a difference in infants' phenomenological experience. That is, with increasing cognitive development, continuity in these early emotional experiences eventually becomes incorporated into a system of understanding about the world. For example, infants with a low threshold for fear may come to view the world as a dangerous place. In this way, temperament and the self-concept are thought to be separate experiences that interact and contribute to early personality development.

Of course, parental perception of and reaction to early individual differences in emotionality may influence the child's self-concept. Malatesta and Wilson (1988) suggest that the contingent response of parents to an infant's state ("You're feeling cranky today, aren't you?" p. 94) is a central factor in the development of self-awareness. This explanation can account for children's understanding of their own basic emotional states (anger, fear, happiness). More general evaluation of the child's emotional state must also play a role in the child's developing self-concept. For example, children who are perceived as "difficult" may come to see themselves as difficult or "bad." Recent research supports this idea by documenting associations between maternal descriptions of child behavior and independent reports from children about their self-concept (Brown, Mangelsdorf, Agathen, & Ho, in press).

In addition to general labeling of emotions, parents also engage in conversation about emotions, even with very young children (Bretherton, Fritz, Zahn-Waxler, & Ridgeway, 1986; Brown & Dunn, 1992; Denham & Kochanoff, 2002). These conversations can furnish valuable information to the child about emotions in general and contribute to better understanding of self and other. For example, Denham, Zoller, and Couchoud (1994) documented a clear association between mothers' emotion language and preschoolers' emotion knowledge. Although their focus was emotion knowledge generally, rather than emotion knowledge about the self specifically, one might easily infer that children who have more frequent and in-depth conversation about emotion might be more likely to have a richer sense of their own emotional experience—which we believe is at the core of the self-concept.

However, not all talk about emotions is positive talk, and when parents express distress about a child's behavior—("you make me upset when you . . . ") the child may experience emotional distress. Infrequent use of this type of socialization technique is probably beneficial for enriching children's understanding of others' emotional experience. However, if parents frequently express emotional distress about a child's behavior, the child may come to feel badly about his or her own attributes. For example, Bretherton and Beeghly (1992) found that by twenty-eight months of age children were able to label emotions in themselves and others. They were even able to make causal statements about internal states ("Grandma mad [because] I wrote on the wall"). This implies that at less than two and a half years of age at least some children are already capable of internalizing that their behavior has caused distress in others.

Personal Narrative: Making and Remaking Selves

Young children not only participate in here-and-now interaction in which they hear themselves labeled and characterized; they also begin to participate in discourse that is displaced from the here-and-now, invoking past, hypothetical, pretend, and future worlds. There is growing evidence that children from a variety of sociocultural backgrounds within and beyond the United States are able to tell conversational stories about their past experience by the second or third year of life and that personal storytelling is a remarkably frequent feature of everyday family life for many children (for reviews, see Miller, Cho, & Bracey, in press; Ochs & Capps, 2001; Shweder et al., in press). When personal storytelling occurs so abundantly, it is woven densely but almost invisibly into the fabric of young children's social experience.

These findings add a developmental twist to the widely held claim that narrative plays a privileged role in self-construction. Not only is personal storytelling a probable cultural universal; not only do multiple sources of narrative-self affinity—(temporal, causal, evaluative, and conversational)— converge in this genre; this powerful tool for making and remaking selves is available to children remarkably early in life.

Stern (1989) argued that once children are able to narrate their experience, a qualitative transformation occurs in the self-constructive process; practical understanding of self is now subject to revision and reconstruction. In other words, with the emergence of a narrative sense of self, children's understanding of self and other derives not just from their experience of moment-by-moment interpersonal encounters but also from their iterative narrations of those encounters, which are themselves embedded in moment-by-moment interpersonal encounters. A mother reprimands her child for not sharing with a sibling. The next day they co-narrate a story about the not-sharing incident. The child has two opportunities to learn who he is, and both are social opportunities, involving negotiation of meaning with his mother. Suppose another co-narration occurs in which the wronged sibling joins in; now the child has yet another opportunity to revisit the not-sharing incident, one that may challenge him to consider multiple perspectives on his behavior. As Vygotskian theory reminds us, before long the child will be able to tell himself stories about the incident, stories that may echo with the voices of mother and sibling. Thus a focus on early narrative yields fresh insight into the process of self-construction by revealing that this process is both highly dynamic and deeply relational. Narrative self-understanding is doubly anchored, in the past and in the present, to relationships with other people. Narrative provides not only a social arena in which children continue to develop a more elaborated self conception but one in which they can consolidate or alter their self understanding by revisiting their past experience.

There are many fascinating questions that need to be addressed to build upon this insight and further our understanding of the social process of self-construction. Some of them have already proved fruitful; others remain to be cultivated. Of the former, we highlight work that examines co-narration between caregivers and young children, identifying differences in caregivers' style of reminiscing and linking them to differences in children's self-understanding. For example, Fivush and her colleagues (Adams, Kuebli, Boyle, & Fivush, 1995; Fivush, 1998) found that parents were more elaborative, confirming, and emotional when reminiscing with daughters than with sons and that these differences continued from forty to seventy months. By the later age, daughters recalled more information from the past, located that information in a more coherent context, and used a more emotion-laden language. Fivush (1998) concluded that these differences have implications for the development of gendered self-concept, including the possibility that girls come to define themselves more strongly in terms of their autobiographical experience (see also Cho, Agathen, Miller, & Mangelsdorf, 2005).

Important as co-narration is, many families offer young children a range of other narrative roles, including listener and overhearer (Fung, Miller, & Lin, 2004; Ochs & Capps, 2001). Although participant structures of this kind afford rich opportunities for children to learn who they are in relation to significant others, they have received relatively little attention from developmental researchers. When parents tell stories of their own past experience to and around children, they model narrative sense making and convey specific messages about themselves. In some communities, people routinely tell stories about young children in their presence (Miller, 1994; Miller, Wiley, Fung, & Liang, 1997). If a child hears repeatedly the story of how thrilled her mother was when she was born, this story may help to consolidate a view of herself as loved and loveable. If she hears many stories in which significant others portray her as standing up for herself, she may come to see herself as a strong and self-assertive person.

Throughout this section, we have alluded to the practice of retelling particular stories. Studies of repeated engagement with stories are critical to understanding the dynamics of narrative sense making. Adults may be haunted, baffled, or sustained for decades by stories from their own and others' lives (Fung, 2003; Gone, 1999; Hudley et al., 2003). As the person tells the story repeatedly to self and other, it accrues layer upon layer of meaning and may be used to maintain a favored interpretation of self or craft a new interpretation. Sometimes stories become a vehicle of radical self-transformation, as in psychotherapy and Alcoholics Anonymous (Holland et al., 1998). Remarkably, children as young as two years of age can develop a prolonged emotional attachments to particular stories, revisiting them again and again for weeks, months, or even years (Alexander, Miller, & Hengst, 2001; Nelson, 1989; Wolf & Heath, 1992). These studies suggest that from the time children enter into narrative sense making they have the capacity to respond differentially to the ordinary narrative flow, seizing certain stories for especially intense engagement and reconfiguring them systematically. But here again, there are very few studies that trace the "natural history" of stories in children's lives, especially over the long run.

Multiple Cultural Practices and Multiple Selves

All of the social arenas that we have described are structured not just at the individual, relationship, and family levels but at the cultural level as well. For example, personal storytelling is culturally differentiated from the beginning (Miller, Cho, & Bracey, in press; Shweder et al., in press). Wherever it occurs, personal storytelling takes on local color, absorbing values, affective stances, and moral orientations. As young children participate routinely in their community's version of personal storytelling, they learn to interpret their experience in culture-specific terms, carving out culture-specific selves.

This work constitutes a bridge to one of the most consistent and intriguing findings emerging from cultural psychology: the cultural plurality of selves (Heine, Lehman, Markus, & Kitayama, 1999). How does this plurality come about? We argue that this process is inherently developmental, implying a plurality of developmental pathways, some toward self-enhancement, some toward self-improvement, some in other directions. We suggest further that these pathways are formed out of parental folk theories, everyday discourses, and routine practices, many of which are likely to be so habitual as to be almost invisible. A major goal of developmental research in the coming years will be to identify these diverse selfways and the alternate pathways they engender. Researchers will have to look beyond emotion words and personal narrative to other self-expressive practices, discourses, and cultural artifacts. T. S. Saraswathi's chapter in this volume on selfways in India takes a major step in this direction.

Conclusion

We have argued that further insight into the social nature of self-construction can be achieved by focusing on social relationships and mundane social practices that are mediated by language and other semiotic systems. These practices encompass not just the dyadic interaction in which caregiver and child communicate directly with one another but also other social configurations, involving multiple others. Children learn about themselves not just by communicating with significant others but also by watching and listening as significant others reveal themselves through talk and nonverbal expression. Because these practices are so frequent, so saturated with multiple meanings, and so densely connected to other practices in the child's world, they become potent resources for self-making, serving simultaneously to create individual, gender, and cultural differences in young children's self-understanding.

References

Adams, S., Kuebli, J., Boyle, P. A., & Fivush, R. (1995). Gender differences in parent-child conversations about past emotions: A longitudinal investigation. *Sex Roles, 33*(5–6), 309–322.

Alexander, K. J., Miller, P. J., & Hengst, J. A. (2001). Young children's emotional attachments to stories. *Social Development, 10*(3), 374–398.

Bowlby, J. (1982). *Attachment and loss, vol. 1: Attachment* (2nd ed.). New York: Basic Books, 1982. (Orig. published 1969)

Bretherton, I. (1991). Pouring new wine into old bottles: The social self as internal working model. In M. Gunnar & L. A. Sroufe (Eds.), *Minnesota symposium of child psychology*, vol. 23 (pp. 1–11). Hillsdale, NJ: Erlbaum.

Bretherton, I., & Beeghly, M. (1982). Talking about internal states: The acquisition of an explicit theory of mind. *Developmental Psychology, 18,* 906–921.

Bretherton, I., Fritz, J., Zahn-Waxler, C., & Ridgeway, D. (1986). Learning to talk about emotions: A functionalist perspective. *Child Development, 55,* 529–548.

Brown, G. L., Mangelsdorf, S. C., Agathen, J. M., & Ho, M. (in press). Young children's psychological selves: Convergence with maternal reports of child personality.

Brown, J. R., & Dunn, J. (1992). Talk with your mother or your sibling? Developmental changes in early family conversations about feelings. *Child Development, 63,* 836–849.

Campos, J. J., Barrett, K. C., Lamb, M. E., Goldsmith, H. H., & Stenberg, C. (1983). Socioemotional development. In P. Mussen (Series Ed.) & M. H. Haith & J. J. Campos (Vol. Eds.), *Handbook of child psychology, vol. 2: Infancy and developmental psychobiology* (pp. 783–915). New York: Wiley.

Cassidy, J. (1988). Child-mother attachment and the self in six-year-olds. *Child Development, 59,* 121–134.

Cho, G. E., Agathen, J. M., Miller, P. J., & Mangelsdorf, S. C. (2005). Mother-child personal storytelling: A contextual perspective on gender socialization. Poster presented at the biennial meeting of the Society for Research on Child Development, Atlanta.

Denham, S. A., & Kochanoff, A. T. (2002). Children's understanding of emotion. In P. T. Salovey & L. Feldman-Barrett (Eds.), *The wisdom of feelings.* New York: Guilford Press.

Denham, S. A., Zoller, D., & Couchoud, E. A. (1994). Socialization of preschoolers' understanding of emotion. *Developmental Psychology, 30,* 928–936.

Eder, R., & Mangelsdorf, S. (1997). The emotional basis of early personality development: Implications for the emergent self-concept. In R. Hogan, J. Johnson, & S. Briggs (Eds.), *Handbook of personality psychology.* Orlando, FL: Academic Press.

Emde, R. N. (1983). The pre-representational self and its affective core. *Psychoanalytic Study of the Child, 38,* 165–192.

Fivush, R. (1998). Gendered narratives: Elaboration, structure, and emotion in parent-child reminiscing across the preschool years. In C. P. Thompson et al. (Eds.), *Autobiographical memories: Theoretical and applied perspectives.* Hillsdale, NJ: Erlbaum.

Fung, H. (2003). When culture meets psyche: Understanding the contextualized self through the life and dreams of an elderly Taiwanese woman. *Taiwan Journal of Anthropology, 1*(2), 149–175.

Fung, H., Miller, P. J., & Lin, L. (2004). Listening is active: Lessons from the narrative practices of Taiwanese families. In M. W. Pratt & B. H. Fiese (Eds.), *Family stories and the life course* (pp. 303–324). Hillsdale, NJ: Erlbaum.

Gone, J. P. (1999). We were through as keepers of it: The 'missing pipe narrative' and gros ventre cultural identity. *Ethos, 27*(4), 415–440.

Harris, P. L. (1989). *Children and emotion: The development of psychological understanding.* Oxford, UK: Blackwell, 1989.

Heine, S. J., Lehman, D. R., Markus, H. R., & Kitayama, S. (1999). Is there a universal need for positive self-regard? *Psychological Review, 106,* 766–794.

Holland, D., Lachicotte, W., Skinner, D., & Cain, C. (1998). *Identity and agency in cultural worlds.* Cambridge, MA: Harvard University Press.

Hudley, E. P., Haight, W. L., & Miller, P. J. (2003). *"Raise up a child": Human development in an African-American family.* Chicago: Lyceum.

LeVine, R. A. (1989). Infant environments in psychoanalysis: A cross-cultural view. In J. W. Stigler, R. A. Shweder, & G. Herdt (Eds.), *Cultural psychology* (pp. 454–474). New York: Cambridge University Press.

Mahler, M. S., Pine, F., & Bergman, A. (1975). *The psychological birth of the human infant: Symbiosis and individuation.* New York: Basic Books.

Malatesta, C. Z., & Wilson, A. (1988). Emotion cognition interaction in personality development: A discrete emotions functionalist analysis. *British Journal of Social Psychology, 27,* 91–112.

Mead, G. H. (1934). *Mind, self, and society from the standpoint of a social behaviorist.* Chicago: University of Chicago Press.

Miller, P. J. (1994). Narrative practices: Their role in socialization and self-construction. In U. Neisser & R. Fivush (Eds.), *The remembering self: Construction and accuracy in the self-narrative* (pp. 158–179). New York: Cambridge University Press.

Miller, P. J., Cho, C., & Bracey, J. (in press). Working-class children's experience through the prism of personal storytelling. *Human Development.*

Miller, P. J., Wiley, A., Fung, H., & Liang, C. (1997). Personal storytelling as a medium of socialization in Chinese and American families. *Child Development, 68,* 557–568.

Nelson, K. (Ed.) (1989). *Narratives from the crib.* Cambridge, MA: Harvard University Press.

Ochs, E., & Capps, L. (2001). *Living narrative: Creating lives in everyday storytelling.* Cambridge, MA: Harvard University Press.

Saarni, C. (1999). *Children's emotional competence.* New York: Guilford Press.

Shweder, R. A., Goodnow, J., Hatano, G., LeVine, R. A., Markus, H., & Miller, P. (in press). The cultural psychology of development: One mind, many mentalities. In W. Damon & R. M. Lerner (Eds.), *The handbook of child psychology* (6th ed.). New York: Wiley.

Sroufe, L. A. (1990). An organizational perspective on the self. In D. Cicchetti & M. Beeghly (Eds.), *The self in transition: Infancy to childhood.* Chicago: University of Chicago Press.

Stern, D. N. (1985). *The interpersonal world of the infant.* New York: Basic Books.

Stern, D. N. (1989). Crib monologues from a psychoanalytic perspective. In K. Nelson (Ed.), *Narratives from the crib* (pp. 309–319). Cambridge, MA: Harvard University Press.

Thompson, R. A. (1998). Early sociopersonality development. In W. Damon (Series Ed.) & N. Eisenberg (Vol. Ed.), *Handbook of child psychology, vol. 3: Social and personality development* (pp. 25–104). New York: Wiley.

Tronick, E. Z. (1989). Emotions and emotional communication in infants. *American Psychologist, 44,* 112–119.

Wolf, S. A., & Heath, S. B. (1992). *The braid of literature: Children's worlds of reading.* Cambridge, MA: Harvard University Press.

Youniss, J. (1980). *Parents and peers in social development: A Sullivan-Piaget perspective.* Chicago: University of Chicago Press.

PEGGY J. MILLER *is professor in the departments of speech communication and psychology at the University of Illinois at Urbana-Champaign. Her areas of expertise include developmental cultural psychology, early socialization, narrative, and ethnographic methods.*

SARAH C. MANGELSDORF *is acting dean of the College of Liberal Arts and Sciences and professor of psychology at the University of Illinois at Urbana-Champaign. Her areas of expertise include early socioemotional development, attachment, temperament, and emotion regulation.*

PART THREE

Development-in-Contexts

7

New research reveals that media use may contribute to shaping not only adolescents' developing beliefs about gender, race, sexuality, and beauty ideals but also their brains and biology.

Children, Adolescents, and the Media: The Molding of Minds, Bodies, and Deeds

L. Monique Ward

Of the many forces shaping American youth, the media are both the most overrated and the most underrated. In response to tragedies such as school shootings or social problems such as rising obesity or teenage pregnancy rates, the media are often blamed as uniquely responsible. It is the violent video games and ubiquitous fast food commercials that have made our children violent and fat. In these instances, the media's role is overexaggerated, with more power being attributed to them than is appropriate. Research has shown that violence, obesity, and sexuality involve complex behaviors determined by multiple factors, among which media exposure is only one. On the other hand, when it comes to regular, everyday attitudes about the world, such as adolescents' beliefs about gender, race, and themselves, the media's role is often overlooked and underestimated. Less public attention has focused on how media use shapes young viewers' beliefs and behaviors in these domains. Yet emerging evidence indicates that the media—everything from television, movies, and magazines to music and the Internet—are likely to be one of the key forces contributing here as well.

Indeed, interest in the media's role in normative development of children and adolescents continues to grow, being led by research in public health, communication studies, medicine, and social and developmental psychology. Whereas new findings are emerging in traditional topics of study (such as media violence), other new work focuses on how media use affects the body, brain, and diverse behaviors. The goal of this chapter is

NEW DIRECTIONS FOR CHILD AND ADOLESCENT DEVELOPMENT, no. 109, Fall 2005 © Wiley Periodicals, Inc.

to highlight new findings in four domains that offer greater understanding of the media's multifaceted implications for the lives of children and adolescents.

Effects on Brain and Body: Looking Beyond Obesity

A traditional concern about media use, and about TV viewing in particular, has been the relative passivity and inactivity inherent in their use. American children aged eight to eighteen are reported to use the media nearly eight hours each day, devoting three hours to TV viewing alone (Roberts, Foehr, Rideout, & Brodie, 1999). In light of these patterns, concern has been raised that a high level of media use may contribute to the obesity epidemic we currently face. This concern has indeed proven to be warranted, with several studies indicating a significant correlation between greater amount of TV viewing and obesity (Crespo et al., 2001; Proctor et al., 2003; Robinson, 2001). For example, Dietz and Gortmaker (1985) found a significant association between time spent watching TV and the prevalence of obesity in three national samples of youths aged twelve to seventeen, even after controlling for prior obesity, race, socioeconomic status, and several other variables.

Yet, beyond issues of weight, new findings suggest other ways in which media use may affect the body. One new direction has been an examination of how media exposure affects the brain. Regardless of the content, exposure to television images has been found to stimulate the brain and thus may well shape its wiring and development. Supporting this notion, Christakis, Zimmerman, DiGiuseppe, and McCarty (2004) found that a greater level of TV viewing at ages one and three was associated with attention problems at age seven, even controlling for several possible confounds (for example, maternal education, cognitive stimulation in the home). This finding suggests possible links between early, extensive TV viewing and attention deficit or hyperactivity disorder, and it draws attention to the potential of TV use to train early—and also subsequent—brain functioning.

A related program of research is investigating the connection between viewers' hormonal level and their exposure to specific types of media. Previous work by Schultheiss and his colleagues demonstrated changes in participant hormonal level when feelings of power and affiliation were aroused. What type of experience and interaction arouses these feelings? To test whether media stimuli might be such a provocateur, Schultheiss, Wirth, and Stanton (2004) exposed participants to a thirty-minute clip from either *The Godfather Part II* or *The Bridges of Madison County,* chosen to arouse feelings of power or affiliation, respectively. Hormonal levels were tested from participants' saliva before and after viewing the clip and were also compared with levels from control participants. Data indicated significant changes in hormonal levels that varied by sex and experimental condition. After viewing the romantic film, men *and* women experienced a rise in their progesterone level relative to the control; men also experienced a dampening of their testosterone level. Change in testosterone level following exposure to *The Godfather Part II* clip depended on baseline level but increased greatly for men already high in testosterone. These findings indicate that media content can alter our endocrine environment, at least temporarily.

The implications for such an effect are extensive. For example, what more lasting changes might result from repeated viewing? What other content could provoke a hormonal response? Could early exposure to sexual images such as those seen in music videos trigger hormones involved in pubertal development (Ward & Merriwether, personal communication)? Further study is needed to begin to untangle the diverse ways in which media use may affect our very biology.

Me Versus Them: Media Effects on Beliefs About Gender and Race

As noted earlier, whereas societal concern about media effects typically focuses on their shaping of *behaviors,* such as aggression, sexual risk taking, and unhealthy eating, media use is also likely to contribute to shaping children's beliefs about themselves and about others around them. One such area concerns basic beliefs about masculinity and femininity. Nearly every media portrayal, scene, and storyline conveys a message about "normative" and expected behaviors of women and men. From these portrayals, much can be learned about what types of women are considered attractive, which male behaviors draw scorn, and which life choices are rewarded. Yet, research finds that the frequently offered characterizations present a *limited* view of gender roles, relying heavily on stereotypes and one-dimensional characters (the ditz, the brute, and so on; for review, see Signorielli, 2001). With only a limited range of roles, looks, and behaviors presented and rewarded in the media, might children's beliefs about femininity and masculinity become equally constrained? Efforts to address this question in the 1970s and 1980s produced the expected results. Focusing on children's beliefs about women's place in the home versus the workforce, this early research documented both correlational and experimental links between heavy TV viewing and viewers' acceptance of stereotypical beliefs about gender (Signorielli, 2001; Ward & Harrison, 2005).

Focusing on different yet related domains of gender, current findings continue to validate the importance of these connections. Drawing from stereotype threat theory, recent research by Davies, Spencer, Quinn, & Gerhardstein (2002) demonstrates how exposure to media stereotypes can undermine women's confidence and performance. Female undergraduates exposed to stereotypical portrayals focusing on women's domesticity expressed less interest in quantitative careers, performed less well on a math test, and avoided math test items in favor of verbal items more so than did female students without this exposure. These findings offer disturbing indication of the detrimental power of negative media stereotypes.

It is not just women who are at risk. Although much of the early work on media ideals and body image focused on the thin ideal and its effect on female viewers (Groesz, Levine, & Murnen, 2002; Ward & Harrison, 2005), increasingly, attention has focused on the effects of the muscular ideal on men's body image. Societal and media pressures regarding men's bodies have increased dramatically over the recent decade, with heavy emphasis on V-shaped bodies with broad shoulders; highly developed arm, chest, and abdominal muscles; and slim waists (Kolbe & Albanese, 1996; Leit, Pope, & Gray, 2001). Research testing the impact of these stringent ideals finds that frequent readers of fitness magazines report greater body image dissatisfaction, drive for muscularity, and social physique anxiety (Duggan & McCreary, 2004; Morrison, Morrison, & Hopkins, 2003). Moreover, experimental exposure to television images of the male body ideal led to greater dissatisfaction with their own musculature among undergraduate men (Agliata & Tantleff-Dunn, 2004). Therefore, new evidence in multiple domains demonstrates a powerful connection between young viewers' media use and their gender and self-ideals.

A second domain of normative beliefs likely to be shaped by media use are those about race. In our highly segregated society, children's opportunities to interact with people of another ethnic group are often limited. This is especially true for whites, who live in neighborhoods that are on average 81 percent white (Frey & Myers, 2002). For many, then, the most regular "contact" with children from other ethnic groups may come through the media. Yet, what might repeated exposure to films such as *Bringing Down the House,* music videos from Snoop Dogg, and video games such as *Grand Theft Auto* teach white and minority youths about race? In these and other media outlets, only a small slice of African American and Latino Americans' lives are depicted as representative of the larger group, with this one slice focusing on gangster culture, crime, and sexual exploitation. Equally important, how might repeated exposure to such portrayals, or to those that totally exclude real people like them, make young minority viewers feel about themselves? This question is especially pressing given that black and Latino youths consume more media than their European American counterparts (Greenberg, Mastro, & Brand, 2002) and may therefore be even more vulnerable to its stereotypical portrayals of race and gender.

Recent work has begun to address these concerns, illustrating that the nature of media effects on minority viewers depends on the form of media and type of viewer connection. For black youths, evidence suggests that media effects differ according to the student's exposure to and connections with black-oriented rather than mainstream media. Among black teens, Ward (2004) demonstrated that greater exposure to mainstream programming and stronger identification with white characters were each associated with *lower* self esteem, while stronger identification with popular black characters was associated with *higher* self-esteem. Similarly, Schooler, Ward, Merriwether, and Caruthers (2004) found that for black undergraduate women greater exposure to programming with predominantly white casts had virtually no effect on their body image whereas greater exposure to programming with predominantly black casts was associated with a more positive body image. These findings suggest that for black youths connecting to the few black media models available may offer some benefits, whereas emulating white models may be more detrimental to their self-conception.

The picture is less positive for Latino youths, however, who encounter few same-group portrayals (outside of Spanish-language programming). Indeed, current analyses indicate that Latinos make up only 6.5 percent of characters on prime-time TV, but 13 percent of the U.S. population (Children Now, 2004). Recent data indicate that among Latino high school and college students, frequent exposure to mainstream programming is associated with lower social self-esteem and lower appearance self-esteem (Rivadeneyra, Ward, & Gordon, 2005). In addition, findings indicate that among Latino high school students exposure to mainstream TV and Spanish-language TV are both associated with greater endorsement of stereotypical gender roles, suggesting they receive a double dosage (Rivadeneyra and Ward, forthcoming). These findings are only a beginning. Further study is needed, especially work that examines Asian viewers, considers potential risk and protective factors, and asks how these portrayals shape young viewers' perceptions of other ethnic groups.

From Beliefs to Behavior: Contributions of Media Sexual Content

A third direction emerging from the field is renewed attention to the media as an agent of sexual socialization. Whereas it is often suggested that the media assume a prominent role in the sexual education of American youth, empirical evidence supporting this premise has been slow to accumulate. Much of the early work consisted either of content analyses documenting the frequency with which sexual references or acts occurred, or small-scale correlational analyses linking media exposure level and student sexual attitudes (for review, see Ward, 2003). In recent years, stemming from concerns about teenaged pregnancy, sexually transmitted infection, and human immunodeficiency virus, renewed attention has focused on possible connections between media use and adolescent sexual *behavior*. Five government-sponsored, large-scale, longitudinal projects examining this issue are now ongoing (National Institute of Child Health and Human Development, 2000), and smaller, innovative work is under way on other fronts.

Emerging from these studies are consistent and surprising *direct* links between adolescent use of media and early sexual behavior. Focusing on participants' sexual media diets, Pardun, L'Engle, and Brown (2005) found that a greater level of exposure to movies and music high in sexual content was a significant predictor of young teens' participation in a range of sexual activities and of their intention to have sexual intercourse in the future.

Similar results were reported by Ward and Friedman (under review), who found that greater exposure to music videos and talk shows, and stronger identification with popular media characters, each predicted a greater level of dating and sexual experience among high school students. Findings from longitudinal data add further strength to these associations. Specifically, Collins, Elliott, Berry, Kanouse, Kunkel, et al. (2004) found that in a national sample of 1,762 teens participant exposure to sexual content at time one was a strong, positive predictor of both their coital initiation one year later and more rapid progression through noncoital sexual activities (among virgins). Looking at more specific sexual behaviors, Wingood et al. (2003) discovered that frequent viewing of music videos at time one was linked with a larger number of sexual partners and higher likelihood of acquiring a new sexually transmitted disease one year later among black female adolescents. These findings paint a compelling picture of the association between adolescents' media use and their actual sexual behavior. To support this research, additional experimental work is needed, as are investigations testing how sexual content is interpreted, how it shapes viewers' perceptions of their sexual experiences, and whether it also affects their sexual communication and contraceptive use.

Prevention and Intervention: Mediation and Entertainment Education

With numerous findings documenting the negative impact of exposure to media violence and to stereotypical portrayals of race, gender, and sexuality, the question that often surfaces is, What positive and proactive steps can be taken to protect our children? Traditionally, responses have centered on the role of parental mediation and coviewing. Here, the notion is that having parents comment on appropriate and inappropriate content while watching TV with their children can help guide the influence of the messages. Although these constructs were initially discussed and tested in the 1970s and early 1980s, renewed attention to this approach and more rigorous experimental investigation demonstrate the benefits of such intervention. In one study, grade school children viewed four TV clips portraying stereotypical gender roles (Nathanson, Wilson, McGee, & Sebastian, 2002). For children in one condition, the experimenter inserted comments contradicting the stereotypical behavior; in another condition, she did not. Results indicated that children in the mediation condition evaluated the program less positively and expressed greater acceptance of nontraditional gender roles for men than did children who received no mediation. Similar results have been obtained in experimental work testing children's responses to media violence (Nathanson, 2004).

However, because many teens consume television and other media in their bedroom (Roberts, et al., 1999), opportunities for this type of intervention may arise infrequently. What if prosocial messages were embedded in the content itself? Over the past five years, renewed effort has been given to testing the possible role of entertainment education, in which health-promoting information is inserted by media makers into actual media storylines (for review, see Singhal & Rogers, 1999). Such efforts have worked extremely well on the international front, offering soap opera viewers and listeners information about family planning and the importance of literacy education (Singhal & Rogers, 1999). In the United States, the Centers for Disease Control and Prevention and the Kaiser Family Foundation have been working with TV producers to achieve similar outcomes. For example, when information about emergency contraception was included in one episode of *ER*, telephone surveys revealed a substantial increase in the number of regular *ER* viewers who could accurately define this method and explain how to access it (Kaiser Family Foundation, 2000). Similarly, when information about the effectiveness rate in condom use was incorporated into an episode of *Friends,* confirmed teen viewers were later more likely than nonviewers to provide accurate information about this statistic (Collins, Elliott, Berry, Kanouse, & Hunter, 2003). These findings highlight the potential of mainstream entertainment media to increase young viewers' knowledge of important public health issues.

Conclusion

With their ability to amplify or neglect aspects of the social world, the American media are a potent socialization force. Although their influence is often either ignored or overblown, the findings summarized here indicate that neither perspective is entirely appropriate. Yes, some concerns about potential harmful consequences are warranted. Evidence indicates that frequent viewing of mainstream TV is associated with obesity, attention problems, body image dissatisfaction, a greater level of sexual experience, and lower self-esteem (among ethnic minority viewers). Findings from experimental paradigms highlight additional concerns, demonstrating that exposure to specific media stimuli can change viewers' hormonal level and decrease women's math performance. At the same time, however, we see that these connections are not guaranteed and do vary according to the specific media content and viewing audience. Indeed, media content infused with prosocial messages generates positive outcomes. Clearly, there are no easy answers to questions surrounding the nature of media influence; these are complex issues. Perhaps the trends highlighted in this review will encourage us all to stay tuned for future developments.

References

Agliata, D. & Tantleff-Dunn, S. (2004). The impact of media exposure on males' body image. *Journal of Social and Clinical Psychology, 23,* 7–22.

Children Now. (2004). Fall colors: 2003–04: Prime time diversity report. Oakland, CA: Children Now.

Christakis, D. A., Zimmerman, F. J., DiGiuseppe, D. L., & McCarty, C. A. (2004). Early television exposure and subsequent attentional problems in children. *Pediatrics, 113*(4), 708–713.

Collins, R. L., Elliott, M. N., Berry, S. H., Kanouse, D. E., & Hunter, S. B. (2003). Entertainment television as a healthy sex educator: The impact of condom-efficacy information in an episode of "Friends." *Pediatrics, 112*(5), 1115–1121.

Collins, R. L., Elliott, M. N., Berry, S. H., Kanouse, D. E. Kunkel, D. K., Hunter, S. B., & Miu, A. (2004). Watching sex on TV predicts adolescent initiation of sexual behavior. *Pediatrics, 114,* e280-e289.

Crespo, C. J., Smit, E., Troiano, R. P., Bartlett, S. J., Macera, C. A., & Andersen, R. E. (2001). Television watching, energy intake, and obesity in U.S. children. *Archives of Pediatrics and Adolescent Medicine, 155,* 360–365.

Davies, P., Spencer, S., Quinn, D., & Gerhardstein, R. (2002). Consuming images: How television commercials that elicit stereotype threat can restrain women academically and professionally. *Personality and Social Psychology Bulletin, 28,* 1615–1628.

Dietz, W. H., & Gortmaker, S. L. (1985). Do we fatten our children at the television set? Obesity and television viewing in children and adolescents. *Pediatrics, 75,* 807–812.

Duggan, S. J., & McCreary, D. R. (2004). Body image, eating disorders, and the drive for muscularity in gay and heterosexual men: The influence of media images. *Journal of Homosexuality, 47,* 45–58.

Frey, W., & Myers, D. (2002). *Neighborhood segregation in single-race and multi-race America: A census 2000 study of cities and metropolitan areas.* Washington, DC: Fannie Mae Foundation.

Greenberg, B. S., Mastro, D., & Brand, J. E. (2002). Minorities and the mass media: Television into the 21st century. In J. Bryant & D. Zillmann (Eds.), *Media effects: Advances in theory and research.* Hillsdale, NJ: Erlbaum.

Groesz, L. M., Levine, M. P., & Murnen, S. K. (2002). The effect of experimental presentation of thin media images on body satisfaction: A meta-analytic review. *International Journal of Eating Disorders, 31,* 1–16.

Kaiser Family Foundation. (2000). Teens and sex: The role of popular television. Fact sheet. Menlo Park, CA: Kaiser Family Foundation.

Kolbe, R. H., & Albanese, P. J. (1996). Man to man: A content analysis of sole-male images in male-audience magazines. *Journal of Advertising, 25*(4), 1–20.

Leit, R. A., Pope, H. G., & Gray, J. J. (2001). Cultural expectations of muscularity in men: The evolution of playgirl centerfolds. *International Journal of Eating Disorders, 29,* 90–93.

Morrison, T. G., Morrison, M. A., & Hopkins, C. (2003). Striving for bodily perfection? An exploration of the drive for muscularity in Canadian men. *Psychology of Men and Masculinity, 4*(2), 111–120.

Nathanson, A. I. (2004). Factual and evaluative approaches to modifying children's responses to violent television. *Journal of Communication, 20,* 321–336.

Nathanson, A. I., Wilson, B. J., McGee, J., & Sebastian, M. (2002). Counteracting the effects of female stereotypes on television via active mediation. *Journal of Communication, 42*(4), 922–937.

National Institute of Child Health and Human Development. (2000). Workshop on sex and the media. Bethesda, MD: National Institute of Child Health and Human Development.

Pardun, C. J., L'Engle, K. L., & Brown, J. D. (2005). Linking exposure to outcomes: Early adolescents' consumption of sexual content in six media. *Mass Communication and Society, 8*(2), 75–91.

Proctor, M. H., Moore, L. L., Gao, D., Cupples, L. A., Bradlee, M. L., Hood, M. Y., & Ellison, R. C. (2003). Television viewing and change in body fat from preschool to early adolescence: The Framingham children's study. *International Journal of Obesity, 27,* 827–833.

Rivadeneyra, R., & Ward, L. M. (in press). From Ally McBeal to *Sabado Gigante:* Contributions of television use to the gender role attitudes of Latino adolescents. *Journal of Adolescent Research.*

Rivadeneyra, R., Ward, L. M., & Gordon, M. (2005). Distorted reflections: Media use and Latino adolescents' conceptions of self. Unpublished manuscript. Normal: Illinois State University.

Roberts, D., Foehr, U., Rideout, V., & Brodie, M. (1999). *Kids and media at the new millennium.* Palo Alto, CA: Henry J. Kaiser Family Foundation.

Robinson, T. N. (2001). Television viewing and childhood obesity. *Pediatric Clinics of North America, 48,* 1017–1025.

Schooler, D., Ward, L. M., Merriwether, A., & Caruthers, A. (2004). Who's that girl? Television's role in the body image development of young white and black women. *Psychology of Women Quarterly, 28,* 38–47.

Schultheiss, O. C., Wirth, M. M., & Stanton, S. J. (2004). Effects of affiliation and power motivation arousal on salivary progesterone and testosterone. *Hormones and Behavior, 46*(5), 592–599.

Signorielli, N. (2001). Television's gender role images and contribution to stereotyping. In D. Singer & J. Singer (Eds.), *Handbook of children and the media* (pp. 341–358). Thousand Oaks, CA: Sage.

Singhal, A., & Rogers, E. M. (1999). *Entertainment-education: A communicative strategy for social change.* Mahwah, NJ: Erlbaum.

Ward, L. M. (2003). Understanding the role of entertainment media in the sexual socialization of American youth: A review of empirical research. *Developmental Review, 23,* 347–388.

Ward, L. M. (2004). Wading through the stereotypes: Positive and negative associations between media use and black adolescents' conceptions of self. *Developmental Psychology, 40,* 284–294.

Ward, L. M., & Friedman, K. (under review). Using TV as a guide: Associations between television viewing and adolescents' sexual attitudes and behavior. *Journal of Research on Adolescence.*

Ward, L. M., & Harrison, K. (2005). The impact of media use on girls' beliefs about gender roles, their bodies, and sexual relationships: A research synthesis. In E. Cole & J. H. Daniels (Eds.), *Featuring Females: Feminist Analyses of Media.* Washington, DC: American Psychological Association.

Wingood, G. M., DiClemente, R., Bernhardt, J., Harrington, K., Davies, S., Robillard, A., & Hook E. (2003). A prospective study of exposure to rap music videos and African American female adolescents' health. *American Journal of Public Health, 93*(3), 437–439.

L. MONIQUE WARD is associate professor of psychology at the University of Michigan.

8

We propose that institutions can serve as a resource to promote civic identity in youth from low-wealth and other settings. We show how recent studies support this proposition and can constructively reorient developmental research and theory.

Intersection of Social Institutions with Civic Development

James Youniss, Daniel Hart

This chapter presents a review of recent findings from youth civic empowerment programs illustrating our thesis that social institutions can serve as a resource that brings out otherwise untapped civic capacities in young people. These data are especially relevant today when the younger generation's purported political disengagement appears to threaten the perpetuation of our democracy. Contemporary youth have been accused of self-ingratiating consumerism accompanied by a shocking deficit in knowledge of civics (Niemi & Junn, 1998) and a shamefully low rate of voting (Jamieson, Shin, & Day, 2002). Concern is exacerbated by other considerations, such as the rising proportion of immigrant and minority youth (Fussell, 2002), loss of quality employment opportunities (Kerckhoff, 2002), and economic and political uncertainty associated with the latest wave of globalization (Youniss et al., 2002).

Although these facts are grounds for serious reflection, they do not justify pessimism about future youth citizenship. Although the media tend to perpetrate unfavorable images of youth as a matter of course (Gilliam & Bales, 2001), a wealth of empirical data recommend a much more balanced view. These studies show that when given adequate resources young people acquire and put to use constructive capacities that allow them to make a positive contribution to the civic realm. We will now review these

This work is partially supported by a grant, on which the authors are collaborating, from the William T. Grant Foundation.

NEW DIRECTIONS FOR CHILD AND ADOLESCENT DEVELOPMENT, no. 109, Fall 2005 © Wiley Periodicals, Inc.

studies, show how they illustrate the role that institutions can play in promoting civic development, and spell out their implications for developmental theory and social policy.

Youth from Low-Wealth Settings

It is no secret that most research on young people from low-wealth neighborhoods has emphasized risk taking and its prevention. Violence, pregnancy, school dropout, drug abuse, and so on make up a list of problems whose prevention has been the focus of research and policy for several decades. This emphasis left little room for other kinds of studies or for the emergence of positive images of these youths. As a result, even when youth accomplishments were made public, adults judged them as exceptions to the rule.

A lesser known body of work that contradicts this negative characterization shows that young people from low-wealth areas are politically competent and morally committed, and when afforded resources they willingly participate in constructive social change. Consider two examples regarding school reform. The common view is that they tend to dislike school, consider it an instrument of social control, and see little long-term gain in cooperating with it (see a critical review by Nasir, 2004). Larson and Hansen (in press) observed low-wealth minority and immigrant youths for four months in an out-of-school youth empowerment program in Chicago. In discussing problems experienced with the schools, students identified inequitable application of the discipline code as a major impediment to their education. Students checked this perception with surveys of their peers, probed the school system to determine how they might bring about change, figured out how to get administrators to listen to their concerns, and successfully lobbied the superintendent to bring about change. These students also organized a summit on school issues and planned a protest of the introduction of a new systemwide high-stakes test.

Sherman (2002) reported similar results from a youth empowerment program in San Francisco. Over a ten-month period, students designed a survey and polled four hundred peers about problems they faced in classes. Finding that physical contact and sexual harassment were prevalent, they organized their peers to define the problems in more detail, used the results to prepare a manual of tactics for dealing with harassment, and proposed new policy before the greater San Francisco school board.

These two examples illustrate several features of the political prowess of low-wealth minority students. First, results demonstrate that these young people can use cognitive skills in constructive fashion—for example, penetrating the hidden dynamics of the school bureaucracy to get their concerns heeded. Second, results show that young people can work collectively to effect positive change, as in organizing rallies, mounting surveys, and packing school board meetings. Third, these youths used political tactics to hold administrators accountable while being guided by moral principles of fairness that promised benefits to all students. Fourth, these studies illustrate what can be accomplished by affording youth adequate resources that encourage constructive behavior.

The key in both studies was well-designed empowerment programs in which leader-mentors with high expectations served as human scaffolding devices. Consequently, nascent competence was brought to the fore through instructional opportunities that encouraged young people to participate forthrightly in their own political fate.

We now highlight each of these features by showing how it is exemplified and extended as themes in other studies.

Cognitive Competence. Zeldin, Camino, and Calvert (2003) synthesized results of studies in which youths were treated as collaborating decision makers with adults. For example, young people who served on the board of directors of 4-H chapters alongside adults were found to make mature decisions that advanced the organization and were not biased toward youth's self-interest. Confirmation of this conclusion came from adult board members who acknowledged youths' contributions, came to see them in a more positive light, and claimed that such responsible behavior sharpened their own decision making.

Collective Action. Pancer, Rose-Krasnor, and Loiselle (2002) described a form of collective political action in which young people met in "youth conferences" to ferret out common problems and devise policies to address them. These conferences, cosponsored by the Canadian government and private enterprise, were designed to encourage young people from diverse backgrounds to discover their common interests and take an active role in national politics. At recent conferences, participants targeted problems of violence, intolerance, ethnic rivalry, work opportunities, and educational reform as issues in need of fresh policy.

Morality. Hart and Fegley (1995) and Youniss and Yates (1997) offered qualitative descriptions of low-wealth youths doing service—for example, volunteering at soup kitchens for the homeless. As a result, young people incorporated moral concerns into their changed self-perception; for instance, they began to question the moral and political choices leading to homelessness (affordable housing, job training, mental health services, and the like).

Organizations as Resources. Checkoway and his students (2003) reported case studies of youth involvement in community organizing in six cities. For example, in Des Moines, Iowa, professional organizers promoted skills that allowed youth to combat drug dealers in a low-wealth neighborhood. The young people used newfound strategies to survey and establish relationships with neighborhood residents, work with government officials, escort children to and from school, clean abandoned buildings, and upgrade the immediate environment. Adult organizers lent young people skills, collective purpose, and encouragement—resources that brought out latent political and moral capacities that were integrated into the youths' sense of self. It is noteworthy that these organizations typically espouse political, philanthropic, or religious traditions that appeal to young people who are in the process of exploring systems of meaning pertinent to identity formation. These organizations, then, help to nourish a basic developmental process that allows youth to identify with past accomplishments and envision an ideal future to which to aspire.

Youth Activism

These data are reminiscent of the 1960s, when youth took an active role in civil rights, antiwar, free speech, campus self-governance, female equality, and environmental movements. From sociological studies we know about the important role played by churches, government agencies, and other organizations in mobilizing youth to partake in social-political change. We know also that of the youths who participated, a high proportion became lifelong activists in local political affairs, social movements, and voluntary associations (Youniss & Hart, 2002). Several longitudinal studies of civil rights activists (McAdam, 1988), antiwar protestors (Jennings, 2002), and even participants in school government (Hanks & Eckland, 1978) attest to this fact. These findings imply that political participation is a potent and lasting form of political socialization that is as valid for activism on the left (Fendrich, 1993) as on the right (Andrew, 1997). Thus the studies mentioned here are seen as having potential significance for individual political development and evolving citizenship in the next generation.

These data also raise the question of whether youth activism driven by moral concern may be dissipating today with the advance of affluence, spread of consumer culture, and emphasis on individualism. Some illustrations suggest a negative answer.

Protest. At meetings of the World Trade Organization and International Monetary Fund, youth participated with other trade unions and other groups in seeking reforms that harm debtor nations at the benefit of already wealthy nations. These protests have obvious moral purpose that supersedes self-interest since the object is just treatment for poor nations. This is illustrated by student groups such as the Student Alliance to Reform Corporations, which claims membership on 130 campuses and argues that unfettered flow of capital has harmed workers in the West while undermining the cultures to which manufacturing has been moved (Spencer, 2000).

Service. According to national surveys, more than half of today's freshmen enter college with experience in community service, with many of these students continuing to do service throughout their college years (Astin, Sax, & Avalos, 1999). A corollary of this phenomenon is the growth of organizations that promote service. For example, City Year (http://www.Cityyear.org) was started ten years ago in Boston to give young people from diverse backgrounds an opportunity to devote an entire year to service as part of their life preparation. In 2004, there were more than one thousand City Year youths in eleven cities, engaged in projects of improving schools and neighborhoods of low-wealth children and families.

Organized Political Activity. The media have highlighted student efforts to monitor relations between Nike and their universities. The movement was sparked by Nike's outsourcing of manufacturing to poor nations with low wages and minimal labor laws. Nike forged billions of dollars' worth of licensing agreements with colleges to clothe athletic teams and sell clothing in campus stores. There are now more than two hundred campuses on which the student alliance has changed the licensing policy, putting pressure on Nike to alter its labor practices.

Demographics and Economics

We have extolled low-wealth and more-advantaged youth's potential to participate thoughtfully and effectively in political choices bearing on their communities. This does not suggest, however, that society need only refrain from interfering with a developmental process that will inevitably flower into civic knowledge and engagement. Rather, we propose that civic knowledge and engagement are constructed within the context of social institutions and social relationships.

Resources to develop youth competence depend in part on the availability and allocation of social and economic capital within the community. YMCAs operate within buildings, 4-H Clubs rely on youth leaders, and so on. One path we pursued (Hart & Atkins, 2002; Hart, Atkins, Markey, & Youniss, 2004) examines how variations in financial and social capital between communities, and between countries, influence the civic development of youth. It is almost self-evident that grinding poverty can hinder the emergence and functioning of democracy. Zakaria's review of research (2001) suggests that democracy rarely flourishes in a culture with a low per capita gross domestic product. Of the many explanations for this finding, we have focused on the roles of *civic knowledge* and *civic participation* (the latter indexed by volunteering) in fostering democracy (Galston, 2001).

Because ramifications of poverty impinge on developmental outcomes, it is reasonable to imagine that acquisition of civic knowledge and participation in civic life may be affected. We found that social capital matters too, in that *youth bulges*—cohorts of youth that are large relative to the number of adults in a community—slow acquisition of civic knowledge. If adults are a source of information about society and the political system, then access to adults is important for youth's acquisition of civic knowledge. Because settings with youth bulges have relatively few adults, we hypothesize that adolescents in these contexts will acquire less civic knowledge, compared with adolescents in contexts with many adults.

Regarding this hypothesis, Hart et al. (2004) reported that per capita GDP was negatively correlated with the average score for a country's fourteen-year-olds on civic knowledge and rate of volunteering. The ratio of youths to adults in a country was also negatively correlated with civics knowledge, but positively associated with volunteering.

Within the United States, a similar pattern was observed in comparisons across neighborhoods. In two studies of representative samples of households in the United States, we found that adolescents in neighborhood with a high ratio of youths to adults knew less about their government than adolescents living in a neighborhood with a low ratio. Neighborhood poverty and the ratio of youths to adults interacted in volunteering. Adolescents in affluent neighborhoods with a high ratio of youths to adults were more likely to volunteer than those in an affluent neighborhood with few youths. However, in extremely poor neighborhoods, a high ratio of youths to adults depressed volunteering.

The potential for youths to become effective citizens depends on investments the society is willing to make in the institutions that support youth development. A society cannot abandon adolescents in low-resource neighborhoods and expect that they will become effective citizens.

Implications for Developmental Theory and Social Policy

This sample of findings yields four ideas pertinent to research and theory regarding civic development.

Developmental Theory. • *The person in public.* Traditional developmental theory deals mainly with the individual either in private (for example, knowledge individuals possess) or in the abstract (say, nonsituated competence). The work on youth civic engagement brings to focus a different individual who operates in the public arena with tension between groups having competing interests. This individual is not so fragile as psychological theory might propose (Barber, 2004). This individual also pursues interests and uses political strategies collectively to advance group aims.

Typical developmental theory says little about young people acting in public. It speaks more of private competence that may or may not eventuate in real political behavior. Standard theory would underestimate the behavior displayed by young people in the studies mentioned here, especially the political behavior of minority youth from low-wealth communities. Traditional research emphasizes their vulnerability, self-indulgence, and inarticulateness. The portrait derived from the work on youth civic engagement, however, highlights their sturdiness, strategic thinking, and concern for justice.

• *Intergenerational collaboration.* Traditional developmental theory stresses youth's quest for emancipation from parents and social traditions. Two decades ago, this view gave way to the recognition that parents remain central figures in a developmental process where parent-adolescent relationships are transformed toward autonomy tempered by mutuality. The foregoing findings extend this insight to the civic realm as youth's political behavior was mediated through collaboration with adults within organizational contexts. For example, youths willingly adopted tactics that group leaders encouraged for the purpose of achieving school reform. In antisweatshop protests, students collaborated with labor unions and intercampus groups to mount a campaign designed to alter licensing policies. These studies demonstrate the importance of youth-adult cooperation and refocus on adults not as objects to shun but as resources whose knowledge can be gainfully shared, and whose moral interests coalesce with those of young people.

• *Social-organizational identity.* Identity is a major focus of youth development. It is typically treated as an individual achievement that leads to clarity rather than diffusion. The studies in question expand this notion to the social and public sides of identity. Young people need not invent systems of meaning anew, because such systems already surround them in the form of political, ethnic, religious, and other traditions. Each comes with known historical accomplishments and pictures an ideal future; each offers a formula for moving from the present to an ideal future. Thus youth is invited to join in the process of making history by adapting systems to the realities that the generation confronts. Civil rights, environmental conservation, and other such movements exemplify how acceptance of the invitation leads to advances in lifelong personal identity and social transformation.

• *Youth as a critical period.* Mannheim (1952) suggested that as youth cohorts meet political history at particular moments, their views of society and politics are colored in a particular way. This marking persists as the cohorts move along the life cycle, maintaining their peculiar orientation. In contrast, most developmental theories of adolescence have favored a kind of phenomenology that prizes the flexible openness of the future; once youths depart from parents, they leave tradition behind to seek an indeterminate future. This position conflicts with our view of social identity and does not square with longitudinal results that link youth engagement with political participation in later adulthood—to wit, the best predictor of adult voting, participation in social movements, and involvement in voluntary associations is the individual's participation in political activities during politically right or left activism during youth.

Conclusion and Implications for Social Policy

We have highlighted the potential of youth to contribute to society's political and moral future. Our review suggests that adolescents can, with provision of adequate resources, be thoughtful and effective participants in the continuous renewal of democratic society. An appreciation of this potential should quell current fears that democracy will fail as today's youth cohort moves into adulthood. Youth's potential reaches fruition with the scaffolding provided by collaborating institutions and relationships. As Alexis de

Tocqueville, still regarded as an astute observer of American civic life, noted, the vibrancy of democracy in the United States was (and is) attributable to citizens' deep civic knowledge, derived through participation:

> An American should never be led to speak of Europe, for he will then probably display much presumption and very foolish pride. He will take up with those crude and vague notions which are so useful to the ignorant all over the world. But if you question him respecting his own country, the cloud that dimmed his intelligence will immediately disperse; his language will become as clear and precise as his thoughts. He will inform you what his rights are and by what means he exercises them; he will be able to point out the customs which obtain in the political world. You will find that he is well acquainted with the rules of administration, and that he is familiar with the mechanisms of the laws. The citizen of the United States does not acquire his practical science and his positive notions from the books; the instruction he has acquired may have prepared him for receiving those ideas but did not furnish them. The American learns to know the laws by participating in the act of legislation; and he takes a lesson in the forms of government from governing. The great work of society is ever going on before his eyes and, as it were, under his hands [Tocqueville, 2004].

Recent research refines and sharpens Tocqueville's insights. We hope that his eloquent insight and our overview of research can deepen our shared commitment to fostering the opportunities for youth to participate in "the great work of society."

References

Andrew, J. A. III (1997). *The other side of the sixties: Young Americans for freedom—the rise of conservative politics.* New Brunswick, NJ: Rutgers University Press.

Astin, A. W., Sax, L. J., & Avalos, J. (1999). The long-term effects of volunteerism during the undergraduate years. *Review of Higher Education, 21,* 187–202.

Barber, B. K. (2004). The pivotal role of the meaning of political violence: Comparing the voice of Palestinian and Bosnian youth. In B. K. Barber (Ed.), *Adolescents and war: How youth deal with political violence.* New York: Oxford University Press.

Checkoway, B., Richards-Schuster, K., Abdullah, S., et al. (2003). Young people as competent citizens. *Community Development Journal, 38,* 298–309.

Fendrich, J. (1993). *Ideal citizens: The legacy of the civil rights movement.* Albany: State University of New York Press.

Fussell, E. (2002). Youth in aging societies. In J. Mortimer & R. Larson (Eds.), *The changing adolescent experience: Societal trends and the transition to adulthood.* New York: Cambridge University Press.

Galston, W. A. (2001). Political knowledge, political engagement, and civic education. *Annual Review of Political Science, 4,* 217–234.

Gilliam, F. D., & Bales, S. (2001). Strategic frame analysis: Reframing America's youth. *Social Policy Report,* no. 15. Ann Arbor, MI: Society for Research in Child Development.

Hanks, R., & Eckland, B. K. (1978). Adult voluntary associations. *Sociological Quarterly, 19,* 481–490.

Hart, D., & Atkins, R. (2002). Civic development in urban youth. *Applied Developmental Science, 6,* 227–236.

Hart, D., Atkins, R., Markey, P., & Youniss, J. (2004). Youth bulges in communities: The effects of age structure on adolescent civic knowledge and volunteering. *Psychological Science, 15,* 591–597.

Hart, D., & Fegley, S. (1995). Altruism and caring in adolescence: Relations to moral judgment and self-understanding. *Child Development, 66,* 1346–1359.

Jamieson, A., Shin, H. B., & Day, J. (2002). Voting and registration in the election of November, 2000. In *Current Population Reports.* Washington, DC: U.S. Census Bureau.

Jennings, M. K. (2002). Generation units and student protest movements in the United States. *Political Psychology, 23,* 303–324.

Kerckhoff, A. C. (2002). The transition from school to work. In J. Mortimer & R. Larson (Eds.), *The changing adolescent experience: Societal trends and the transition to adulthood* (pp. 52–87). New York: Cambridge University Press.

Larson, R., & Hansen, D. (in press). The development of strategic thinking: Learning to impact human systems in a youth activism program. *Human Development.*

Mannheim, K. (1952). *Essays on the sociology of knowledge* (P. Kecskemeti, Ed.). London: Routledge Kegan Paul.

McAdam, D. (1988). *Freedom summer.* New York: Oxford University Press.

Nasir, N. S. (2004). When culture is not in the students, and learning is not in the head. *Human Development, 47,* 108–116.

Niemi, R. G., & Junn, J. (1998). *Civic education: What makes students learn?* New Haven, CN: Yale University Press.

Pancer, S. M., Rose-Krasnor, L., & Loiselle, L. D. (2002). Youth conferences as contexts for engagement. In B. Kirshner, J. L. O'Donoghue, & M. McLaughlin (Eds.), *Youth participation: Improving institutions and communities* (pp. 47–64). San Francisco: Jossey-Bass.

Sherman, R. F. (2002). Building young people's lives: One foundation's strategy. In B. Kirshner, J. L. O'Donoghue, & M. McLaughlin (Eds.), *Youth participation: Improving institutions and communities* (pp. 65–82). San Francisco: Jossey-Bass.

Spencer, J. (2000). Raising a ruckus: Students take the bus to DC. *The Nation,* Apr. 24. Available at http://web2.uwindsor.ca/flipside/vol3/apr00/ooap22a.htm.

Tocqueville, A. D. (2004). *Democracy in America* (H. Reeve, trans.). New York: Library of America. (Orig. published 1835).

Youniss, J., Bales, S., Christmas-Best, V., Diversi, M., McLaughlin, M., & Silbereisen, R. (2002). Youth civic engagement in the twenty-first century. *Journal of Research on Adolescence, 12,* 121–148.

Youniss, J., & Hart, D. (2002). Motivation, values, and civic participation. Civic engagement working paper no. 1. College Park: University of Maryland, Democracy Collaborative: Knight Foundation Civic Engagement Project.

Youniss, J., & Yates, M. (1997). *Community service and social responsibility in youth.* Chicago: University of Chicago Press.

Zakaria, F. (2001). The politics of rage: Why do they hate us? *Newsweek,* Oct. 15, p. 22.

Zeldin, S., Camino, L., & Calvert, M. (2003). Toward an understanding of youth in community governance. Social policy report, no. 17. Ann Arbor, MI: Society for Research in Child Development.

JAMES YOUNISS is Wylma R. and James R. Curtin Professor of Psychology at Catholic University of America.

DANIEL HART is professor of psychology at Rutgers University.

9

The areas considered in this chapter have to do with the
aims of family socialization, the nature of influence,
linking multiple sources of influence, and the range
of families and contexts used as a basis for accounts of
socialization. In each area, moving beyond restrictive
assumptions opens up new ways of thinking and new
research questions.

Family Socialization: New Moves and Next Steps

Jacqueline J. Goodnow

Within analyses of family socialization, new directions are currently taking
many forms. Some have to do with the nature of influence (who has what
effect, and how effects come about). Others have to do with new ways of
viewing what develops, and with the extent to which our current views rest
on a narrow range of families and social contexts.

This brief chapter considers some of those challenges and changes, with
an emphasis how to take them further. With regret, the material chosen—
the references especially—must exclude much of what might be covered. I
have opted, however, for material that combines conceptual frameworks with
researchable questions and that has implications for understanding both the
nature of influences and the nature of what develops.

Structurally, the material is in four sections. Each considers some constraining positions and alternatives that offer new directions. The first raises
questions about the aims of socialization. It focuses on moving beyond
behavior toward parents and agreement with others. The second raises
questions about the nature of influence. It focuses on moving beyond a pre-
occupation with some particular ages (early childhood and adolescence)
and with methods of control. The third has to do with linking multiple
sources of influence (parents plus peers, schools, neighborhoods, and so
on). The fourth takes up moves toward widening the range of families and
contexts that we use as a basis for our views of socialization.

NEW DIRECTIONS FOR CHILD AND ADOLESCENT DEVELOPMENT, no. 109, Fall 2005 © Wiley Periodicals, Inc.

Aims of Socialization

Accounts of socialization often read as if the only goals involved were correct behavior toward parents, or more broadly, agreement with the values of an older generation. Positions of this kind limit our perspectives and call for expansion.

Moving Beyond Emphasis on Behavior or Attitude Toward Parents. Orientation toward parents covers only part of the socialization picture. In real life, parents with more than one child (the majority of cases) spend a remarkable amount of time—more than what research studies reflect—promoting particular relationships among siblings: share, yield, don't squabble, don't fight, look after each other, remember you're the oldest, and so forth. Parents also often emphasize the need to understand that "we're a family," and children come to understand that obligations are part of family life (compare Fuligni, 2001).

Emphasis on parent-child dyads has also led to the relative neglect of how socialization is often targeted toward collective identity. To take one example, many children in this world learn to see themselves as members of a church or a faith that tells them how to behave and supports them at times of crisis. A study by Hudley, Haight, & Miller (2003) is a superb beginning on this topic. We are also starting to pay more attention to how children acquire a view of the world outside the family. Parents, it is increasingly recognized, do promote in their children a recognition that some "others" are not always positively inclined toward the group to which they belong, together with awareness of how to cope with negative encounters (see Hughes & Chen, 1999, on "racial socialization"). We need to know more about those aspects of socialization and, in a less defensive manner, add to them the promotion of a child's understanding of "how the system works" (in effect, the early development of "cultural capital").

Are there ways of bringing together what may be aimed for or learned that cover people both within and outside the family? It would be a source of regret if we were left with separate pieces (behavior toward parents, toward siblings, toward teachers, and so on). A promising way forward, I suggest, lies in regarding what develops as an understanding of relationships and of the situations where one kind of relationship is expected rather than another. Fiske (1991), for example, has divided "orientations to social life" into those marked by communal sharing, authority ranking, exchange, and market pricing, each with "implementation rules" in a variety of situations. He regards the four orientations as universal. Children or newcomers, however, need to understand the specific people or the specific situations that in any cultural setting go with each orientation.

How that understanding develops is as yet largely unknown. Developmentalists could well turn to filling this gap, capitalizing on the current availability of several methods for determining what kinds of "category errors" are likely to be made and which errors are regarded as more serious than others (compare Haslam, 2004). Treating person X in communal fashion rather than in a way that respects a difference in status or authority, for example, is a category error. Calling parents by their first names, to take a family example, is regarded as a serious category error in some families but not in others.

Moving Beyond Compliance, Acceptance, or Agreement. Many studies of socialization read as if the mark of achievement is a younger generation's agreement with what parents or people in authority value. This bias, however, again overlooks several aspects of family life. Parents, for example, care about agreement in some areas but not in others (disagreement is not necessarily conflict; Goodnow, 1996a). Parents also encourage children to understand areas and forms of compromise, leeway, and negotiation, together with points that represent limits. They mark some issues as not negotiable, as "not on." They mark some ways of negotiating or of saying no as acceptable, others as not. In some areas, they are willing to compromise or shift goals. In others, they put in extra effort to achieve their initial aims.

The challenge now is to locate areas where we can observe these aspects of socialization. One possibility is school achievement. For a further area, my colleagues and I have turned to contributions to the work of a household (Goodnow, 1996b). This has turned out to be an area where children learn a great deal about styles of contribution and negotiation, about what must be done and what can be delayed, downsized, varied, or delegated. Hours for going to bed or coming home, styles of dress, visits to relatives: these seem likely to provide others.

Nature of Influence

As constraining influences, I single out an emphasis on some limited ages, and on parental methods of control. For both, new directions are feasible.

Moving Beyond Restricted Ages. Studies of socialization are typically concerned with changes within young children and adolescents, chosen perhaps because these are phases where issues of control, supervision, and compliance are seen as salient.

Why go further? The reasons are several. The restriction ignores the reality of family life: parents continue their socialization effort well beyond adolescence. It limits any developmental picture of how socialization efforts change over time. It ignores also the conceptual need to consider both socialization efforts that establish a pattern and efforts that maintain it. We seem often to proceed as if early accomplishments will inevitably be self-sustaining.

How to go further? One way is to trace changes over time in how parents and children deal with issues that do not go away (tension among siblings, ways of speaking, approaches to food). A second is to ask how and when parents aim for outcomes that will be effective over time. They may, for example, encourage children to be future-oriented, or aim for the children helping themselves to maintain a path, teaching them methods of recovery or repair. They may also work toward children being willing to disclose to parents what they do or what they encounter, long before disclosure becomes critical. A third is to explore directly how parents regard aspects of timing: what they regard, for example, as "solid" or as needing to be sustained from time to time, together with the times when extra effort is seen as no longer effective (for better or worse, the parent's job is felt to be finished).

A fourth and last direction is ask what makes assumptions about "early experience" or "early socialization" so attractive. I can understand, for example, their appeal to politicians. They can then direct all their funding efforts toward "the early years" and "parent education," ignoring the importance of later transition points, shifts in path, second chances, recovery routes, parental resources, or neighborhood effects. Psychologists, however, also seem prone to see life as determined only by how the twig is bent, and that proneness calls for closer analysis than it has so far received.

Reconsidering How Influences Have Effects. Within psychological studies of parents' involvement in socialization, there is much literature on the significance of parental methods. They range from forms of discipline, modeling, guidance, and coaching to shaming, teasing, and a mixture of warmth and control. There is also a smaller literature on the significance of family routines and on the information-processing steps by which parental messages are perceived and possibly accepted. The chapters in Grusec and Kuczynski (1997) give examples.

Which promising directions to select? Partly because of space and partly because it brings along some diversity in direction, I focus on a particular kind of effect: one often called "internalization."

To start with, we need to distinguish between two meanings of the term. The first is the sense that the views one comes to hold or the practices one comes to follow are based on one's own decisions. Like intrinsic motivation, they are not felt to be imposed or taken over from others. This meaning is prominent in analyses of some particular parental methods and qualities (such as promotion of a sense of choice and the warmth of the parent-child relationship).

The second is the sense that some views or practices are right, natural, not optional, and in no need of reflection or questioning. This meaning is more prominent in analyses of the effect of cultural models or cultural practices (cultural in the sense that most people in a social group follow the same ways of thinking or acting). Gender distinctions and ways of "doing gender" are the classic examples.

The second meaning is the one I see as especially worth exploring (the chapters in Goodnow, Miller, & Kessel, 1995, provide several examples of doing so, with an emphasis on practices). Still largely missing, however, is any rich account of how shared views or practices lead on to a sense of what is natural or morally right.

To bring this out, one possibility consists of asking whether all people matter equally. Shared views and practices may matter most when the others are people to whom an individual is attached. Another consists of asking how dissent is handled. A child's doubts or questions may be responded to with interest or horror. An individual may also be "cocooned" from encounters with dissenting others, or encouraged to discount the value of their views and practices. These others may be treated, for example, as odd, insignificant, not trustworthy, nonbelievers, or best avoided. In effect, both within and outside the family we can begin to give more attention than is currently given to how a sense of the natural, the outrageous, and the impossible is developed.

Linking Multiple Sources of Influence

Analyses of socialization have always held an interest in several sources of influence. Developmental psychology, for example, has added fathers to a mothers-only picture, and siblings, grandparents, and kin to a parents-only picture. It has also moved beyond biological ties, adding peers, child care centers, neighborhoods, patterns of paid work, legal systems.

Those additions, however, tend to generate concepts of linkage that are seldom brought together. Adding fathers to a mothers-only picture, for instance, generated the concept of first- and second-order effects. Adding paid work to family life generated concepts such as "spillover." Adding child care and schools generated interest in the consistency of messages from one source to another. We need now to ask how far dimensions and concepts used for one combination apply to others (Goodnow, in press).

At the same time, the main proposals offered for linking several sources call for further work. I single out two. First, we can consider links in *additive or subtractive terms*. Additive terms have been prominent in cultural analyses of socialization, mainly in the form of questions about the extent and the effects of people in a social group sharing the same mode of viewing the world or the same routine practices (the effects of such sharing are not always seen as positive). Subtractive, competitive, or oppositional terms, with assumed negative effects, have been prominent within developmental psychology. Peers, for example, are often seen as diminishing the influence of parents. Paid work impoverishes the quality of parenting. Child care may diminish the consistency of socialization messages. We need now to ask when and to what the two models apply.

Second, we can regard several influences as "surrounds" for each other. Bronfenbrenner's visual metaphor of concentric circles (1979) is a well-known example. It presents, however, a relatively static and segmented picture. How, for example, do these various sources of influence affect one another? Can we go beyond connections in the form of spillover, or in the form of "trickle down and bubble up"? Can we regard parents as forming more than a barrier between children and neighborhoods: blocking, interpreting, or mediating "outside" events?

One way forward, I suggest, is to consider multiple sources in terms of systems or patterns. Within family systems theory, for example, family members are regarded as forming alliances or patterns of relationships with one another. They are also seen as able, in varying degrees, to substitute for one another when the need arises. We can translate those concepts into questions about influences from "inside" and "outside" the family and about their interconnections. We can ask, for example, which people or agencies are seen as possible substitutes for parental influence or control (from grandparents to child minders or the state). Who acts as a substitute in various circumstances? When and how is a temporary substitution (as during the absence of a parent) expected to end?

In a related move, we can consider various sources of influence in terms of areas of expected responsibility. Who, for instance, can cover topics such as sex education? Is advice acceptable only if first invited? What do parents see as parental areas of responsibility as against the responsibility of others or of individuals themselves? What do they see as occasions for a sense of "well done" or of regret that they did not exert extra effort or find the magic method that others seem to have found? Where do they see their effort as especially needed if children are not to go "astray"? How do they and others account for parental effort having had less success than was hoped for?

We can also extend this kind of move to considering children's understanding of various sources of influence. To take one example, children clearly have at an early age some understanding of who can claim various kinds of influence or authority (consider the response "You're not my mother" to some directives from siblings or other adults). The changing forms that understanding takes, and its course of development, are still relatively unknown.

In effect, we can use links in the form of areas of perceived responsibility or rights, and the perceived possibilities of replacement or substitution, to open up specific research questions about what adults have in mind, what children encounter, and what children come to understand or regard as right and proper.

Expanding the Range of Families and Contexts Considered

Interest is increasing in how approaches to socialization vary both within and across cultural groups and in the need to move beyond a view of other groups as simply "departures from the norm" or exotic variations on what should occur. An example is the change in one journal's title from *Journal of Marriage and the Family* to *Journal of Marriage and Family*. Others are to be found in the chapters within a new work by Cooper, Garcia Coll, Bartko, Davis, and Chapman (in press). The book treats diversity as a conceptual resource for the study of development rather than as a source of noise or a barrier to development of general theory. It also calls for attention to how children can use their distinctiveness as a strategic resource rather than simply suffer it as a disadvantage, and to differences within cultural or social groups as well as across them.

At this point, there is no longer a need to continue demonstrating that diversity exists. The questions that now stand out take the form: What functions does attention to diversity serve? What further groups would now best serve those functions?

That several functions are served is not in doubt. Attention to some social groups, for example, can break down their invisibility or their being regarded as separate from the mainstream It can also break down the assumption that there is only one route to becoming a responsible adult, or that some parental methods have universal effects (for instance, the assumption that "authoritarian" parenting always goes with a lack of warmth and developmental damage).

The issue now is one of choosing groups on a thought-through basis. Convenience and surface novelty ("no one has worked with this group before")—are no longer sufficient reasons for choice. The choice may instead be on the basis that some groups use methods of influence that shake our own theories of what helps, what harms, and what should be aimed for. It may also be on the basis that some groups bring out with particular clarity the nature of the challenges that families face and how they try to meet them. How to maintain a sense of continuity and persistence (as an individual, a family, or a cultural group) in the face of family change and social change, for example, is the basis to the choice by Chandler, Lalonde, Sokol, and Hallett (2003) of First Nations in Canada as a focus. In effect, the bases for choice may vary. We need, however, to direct our choices toward particular gaps or assumptions within current research and theories.

Conclusion

There is no shortage of new directions possible. I have singled out four areas that strike me as particular sites of change. They are clearly marked by a pervasive concern with finding ways to take into account both families and the larger social contexts of which children and their parents or siblings take an active part. Others would probably make another set of choices. The challenges that emerge, however, are likely to be the same: filling gaps, linking pieces, moving beyond restrictive assumptions, and using conceptual shifts to open up new and researchable questions. Exciting times, indeed.

References

Bronfenbrenner, U. (1979). *The ecology of human development: Experiments by nature and design.* Cambridge, MA: Harvard University Press.

Chandler, M. J., Lalonde, C. E., Sokol, B. W., & Hallett, D. (2003). Personal persistence, identity development, and suicide. *Monographs of the Society for Research in Child Development, 68*(2, whole no. 273).

Cooper, C., Garcia Coll, C., Bartko, T., Davis, H., & Chapman, C. (eds.) (in press). *Hills of gold: Rethinking diversity and contexts as resources for children's developmental pathways*. New York: Oxford University Press.

Fiske, A. P. (1991). *Structures of social life: The four elementary forms of human relations*. New York: Free Press.

Fuligni, A. (2001). Family obligation and academic motivation of adolescents from Asian, Latin American, and European backgrounds. In A. J. Fuligni (Ed.), *Family obligation and assistance during adolescence: Contextual variations and developmental implications*. New Directions for Child and Adolescent Development, no. 94 (pp. 61–76). San Francisco: Jossey-Bass.

Goodnow, J. J. (1996a). Acceptable ignorance, negotiable disagreement: Alternative views of learning. In D. Olson & N. Torrance (Eds.), *Handbook of psychology in education* (pp. 345–368). Oxford, UK: Blackwell.

Goodnow, J. J. (1996b). From household practices to parents' ideas about work and interpersonal relationships. In S. Harkness & C. Super (Eds.), *Parents' cultural belief systems* (pp. 313–344). New York: Guilford.

Goodnow, J. J. (in press). Contexts, diversity, pathways: Linking and expanding with a view to theory and practice. In C. R. Cooper, C. Garcia Coll, T., Bartko, H., Davis, & C. Chapman (Eds.), *Hills of gold: Rethinking diversity and contexts as resources for children's developmental pathways*. New York: Oxford University Press.

Goodnow, J. J., Miller, P. J., & Kessel, F. (Eds.) (1995). *Cultural practices as contexts for development*. New Directions for Child Development, no. 67. San Francisco: Jossey-Bass.

Grusec, J. E., & Kuczynski, L. (Eds.) (1997). *Handbook of parenting and the transmission of values*. New York: Wiley.

Haslam, N. (2004). *Relational models theory: Advances and prospects*. Hillsdale, NJ: Erlbaum.

Hudley, E.V.P., Haight, W., & Miller, P. J. (2003). *"Raise up a child": Human development in an African-American family*. Chicago: Lyceum.

Hughes, D., & Chen, L. (1999). The nature of parents' race-related communications to children: A developmental perspective. In L. Balter & C. S. Tamis-LeMonda (Eds.), *Child psychology: A handbook of contemporary issues* (pp. 467–490). Philadelphia: Psychology Press/Taylor and Francis.

JACQUELINE J. GOODNOW *is a professorial research fellow in the Department of Psychology, Macquarie University, Sydney, Australia.*

10

Although research on friendship reveals the significance of friendship for children, questions about friendship and development remain unanswered. It is argued that the study of friendship would benefit from a return to basic questions about what friendship is, how it is measured, and how it varies across people and contexts.

Friendship and Development: Putting the Most Human Relationship in Its Place

William M. Bukowski, Lorrie K. Sippola

The study of friendship has been an enduring mainstay of research on developmental psychology. For more than a century, developmental psychologists have focused their attention on the features, processes, and effects of children's friendship relations. (In this chapter, *children* refers to children and adolescents.) Influenced by the theoretical perspectives of many theorists (among them Sullivan, 1953), an abundance of research has clearly demonstrated that (1) friendships are characterized by qualities that distinguish them from other types of relationships (that is, they are voluntary in nature); (2) some children are more likely to have a "friend" than others; and (3) under certain conditions friendship relations can create important, if not vital, opportunities for healthy social and emotional development. Thus, the goal of much of research has been to understand the place of friendship in the context of human development. Despite the important contribution that this research has made to understanding the role of friendship in human development, the results of most research have not been as strong as suggested by the rich, theoretical frameworks offered by Sullivan

Work on this chapter was supported by grants from the Social Sciences and Humanities Research Council of Canada to both authors and by a grant from the Fonds Québécois de la Recherche sur la Société et la Culture to the first author. Correspondence to the first author should be directed to the Department of Psychology and Centre for Research in Human Development, Concordia University, 7141 ouest, rue Sherbrooke, Montréal, Québec, Canada, H4B 1R6.

and others. In this chapter, we suggest that the lack of strong findings is primarily due to the challenges confronting researchers who are attempting basically to capture an elusive phenomenon. Thus, an essential premise underlying this chapter is that to further advance this understanding, it is essential that researchers move beyond examining the place of friendship in human development by putting more effort into understanding friendship "in its place."

This chapter has two parts. One looks back to see how friendship has been treated by theorists and in past research, and the other looks forward to see how the study of friendship might be enriched by new ideas, new strategies, and new approaches. Our basic point is that although the study of friendship has flourished and has produced several fundamental hypothesis-confirming findings, friendship research would benefit from going back to its conceptual roots—but by expanding its consideration of what friendship is and how it "happens." We propose that by going back to think broadly about the "stuff" of friendship, research on friendship can move forward to reveal its significance for human development.

Ideas About Friendship

Friendship has been ascribed with many properties and features. Typically a set of interrelated ideas as to the stuff of friendship has been relied on to justify or motivate research on friendship. From these views, friendship has been seen as an opportunity to obtain both instrumental and psychosocial provisions (see, for example, Furman & Robins, 1985). On the basis of descriptions of friendship seen in the writing of philosophers such as Aristotle, as well as in children's descriptions of friendship, researchers have seen it as offering many opportunities: for help and protection; to have pleasant and stimulating experiences such as companionship and shared participation in activities; to have powerful and positive emotional experiences such as acceptance, closeness, and intimacy; and to have self-affirming experiences such as loyalty, security, and reflected appraisal (see Bukowski, Hoza, & Boivin, 1994). Inherent in the notion of provision is the idea that friendship offers the stuff required to satisfy human needs.

A related theme in theory and research on friendship is the idea that it lies at the interface between self and other. According to this approach, the self is affected (or even created) by the presence of and experience with a friend, and through friendship one becomes especially aware of and sensitive to the needs of others (Youniss & Smollar, 1985). The claim is that through one's interaction with a friend one has not only opportunities for the positive and stimulating experiences that derive from companionship but unique opportunities to learn how one is seen by a caring and equal other. By experiencing this degree of acceptance and validation from one's friend, the self is believed to be enhanced in both valence (it becomes more positive) and content (one's strengths and weaknesses are clarified). Central to this concept of friendship is that the effects of friendship are due to specific processes occurring at the interface between self and the other.

These ideas regarding the significance and power of friendship to shape the self and influence adjustment are typically found in the writings of a group of philosophers known as the symbolic interactionists (Cooley, 1909; Mead, 1934) and in the work of Sullivan (1953). Harry Stack Sullivan in particular had an idyllic, or even utopian, vision of friendship. He conceived of it as something that was simple and powerful. His conception was simple in the sense that he devoted little attention to the dynamics or processes of friendship. It was powerful in that the simple dynamics he saw in friendship would have the strength to allow a youngster to overcome or compensate for problems resulting from negative experiences in other aspects of social relations with peers or in the family. Sullivan believed that the essential features of friendship were its affective bond and the opportunities it offered for reflected appraisal. For Sullivan, these affect-based experiences were the stuff of friendship; it was these experiences that would account for the effects of friendship.

These ideas have motivated many projects aimed at testing the hypothesis that friendship brings with it positive effects on well-being. Findings from such studies have been chronicled in many books and review papers (Newcomb & Bagwell, 1995; Hartup, 1996; Rubin, Bukowski, & Parker, in press). Taken together, findings show that friendship can (1) be an important correlate of affective and behavioral well-being, (2) function as a counterweight to offset the effects of negative peer experiences such as rejection, (3) moderate the effects of risk on outcomes such as victimization, and (4) compensate for nonoptimal experiences within the family. Typically, the evidence indicates that in many ways children with friends are better off than children without them. Despite the general evidence that friendship is associated with well-being, specific findings are often weaker than what one would expect given the apparent power that theorists have claimed for friendship. Moreover, the particular concepts or variables that are assessed in these studies do not always match the features that theorists have ascribed to friendship. Certainly, most reported findings are consistent with hypotheses taken from one theory of friendship or another. But for the most part they tell us little about what theorists have suggested is the stuff of friendship—that is, about what friendship is, how it works, and what it means to children as they are growing up.

Friendship Goes Back to the Future

From our point of view, friendship research can and should be more lively than it currently is. We propose that to make the study of friendship richer, more revealing, and more rewarding, those who study friendship and development need to return to a set of basic questions about what it is, how it should be measured, and how and why it varies across children and contexts.

Perhaps most important, those who study friendship need to be clearer and think more broadly about what the stuff of friendship is.

As with the study of any construct, issues of measurement and operationalization need to be tightly linked with theory. With friendship, these issues may be even more critical than usual owing to the complex nature of friendship and the rich but divergent theoretical background that serves as the conceptual ground for friendship research. Friendship researchers appear to generally agree that it must be assessed according to multiple criteria. Typically, the measurement of friendship involves at least two of three questions summarized by Hartup (1996): (1) Is a child part of a friendship? (2) What characteristics do the child and the friend bring to the friendship? and (3) What are the qualities or properties of the friendship relation? That is, the most basic assessment indicates whether a child has a friend and assesses what the friendship is like. This approach is advantageous because it gives both conceptual and methodological structure to research on friendship and has been a source of common ground among friendship researchers. Indeed, it is hard to argue with an approach that is reasoned, compelling, and simple.

Nevertheless, the study of friendship may be hampered by this simplicity and generality, especially in underestimating the complexity and specificity of the theories that motivate friendship research. In other words, by looking for areas of agreement in measuring friendship, researchers avoided the bigger and more important questions about its features. At the outset of this chapter, several points of view regarding the central features of friendship were briefly presented. Most of them make claims about the particular processes or phenomena that give friendship its developmental significance. One would think that it is these exact processes or phenomena that are to be indexed as part of a measure of friendship. It appears, though, that as researchers we have grown comfortable, probably too comfortable, using the measures of friendship already described as proxies for what we think is going on in children's relationships with friends. To make progress, we need to do a better job of putting the stuff of friendship into our friendship measures.

One place to start might be to go back to the original ideas of Sullivan and others who saw friendship as a security system. Before the concept of security became indelibly linked to attachment research, it was seen by Sullivan as the key component of friendship that produced its protective function. The view that friendship's most essential characteristic is its affordance for security is not limited to Sullivan but is seen also in the writings of Blatz (1966) along with other early writing from attachment theorists (Mary Ainsworth's dissertation looked at security with both parents and peers). In light of this, it is not surprising that most efforts to assess friendship quality scales (Parker & Asher, 1993; Bukowski et al., 1994) have included a measure of security. Nevertheless, these scales have often been mixed in with measures of other dimensions of friendship to create an omnibus index. As a result, the effects that are due uniquely to security, or to any other aspect of friendship, cannot be assessed directly. By looking at specific features of friendship, rather than relying on general measures indicating whether a friendship exists, our understanding of the place of friendship in development will become more specific as well.

Certainly, assessing security as a feature or an outcome of friendship is important, but understanding how security emerges along with the role it plays in the day-to-day stuff is equally important. Taking this sort of process-oriented approach requires a change in how friendship is studied. Instead of seeing it as either a predictor or an outcome, research has to focus on its internal dynamics and events. One promising approach to achieving this goal can be seen in a qualitative study conducted by Way, Gingold, Rotenberg, and Kuriakose (2005). They assessed how adolescents from various ethnic groups *experience* security, intimacy, and trust in their friendships. Using an interview format, they asked adolescents to talk about their friendships and examined how the events of the friendships affected their sense of well-being. Way and her colleagues showed, for example, that adolescents, especially from low SES families, used instances of trust such as the sharing of money or secrets to test their friendships in regard to dimensions of closeness, strength, or security. The adolescents they interviewed were clear that they saw friendship as a means of protecting the self and that the experience of being protected by a friend added to their sense of connection with the friend. Brave and focused researchers will follow the example of Way et al. by examining how the processes of friendship unfold and how they are linked to other dynamic aspects of the friendship relation.

Other researchers may decide that an even braver approach is needed to help us understand the basic properties of friendship and their developmental significance. Beyond the usual suspects that are typically cited to justify and inform research on friendship, there are writers and theorists from other disciplines who have offered insights into friendship. Philosophers, both ancient and modern, have written about friendship especially with respect to the properties that define it and according to what it means to be someone's friend, what one owes to a friend, and what it means to share one's life with others (see Badhwar, 1993). Others have tried to point to the challenges, stresses, and struggles that may be inherent to friendship, especially the challenge of negotiating a balance between one's needs and those of the other (Horney, 1950). It is not that these writers do not or cannot have an idyllic or utopian view of friendship. They are simply realistic enough about friendship's human dimensions to see that it can be a challenge as well as an achievement.

These comments make it clear that ideas about friendship are not lacking. We only need to do a better job of findings ways of putting these ideas into practice in research. This challenge might be less daunting than it first seems. Already the themes of self and other that play a central role in the ideas of philosophers and in the writings of theorists such as Horney are apparent in the literature on friendship. Despite the general recognition that friendship involves the self and the other, the fundamental conceptualization of friendship is rarely used directly to study friendship. It may be that these questions are currently not well suited to the quantitative measures and designs that are often used to study friendship. Qualitative researchers, however, have shown that these processes can be assessed in studies with children and early adolescents. Azmitia, Ittel, and Radmacher (2005) used qualitative methods to assess the association between friendship and identity formation. They examined the role of friendship as a "comfort zone" for exploring identity, especially as it might differ for children with high and low self-esteem. An important finding of their study was that low self-esteem impeded development of healthy or good-quality friendships. Whereas boys and girls with low and high self-esteem were observed to have similar thoughts and ideas about friendship, they appeared to manage their friendships very differently. Low-self-esteem boys and girls, for example, appeared to put the needs of their friends ahead of their own and as a result endured prolonged association with high-risk peers.

This new direction taken by Azmitia et al. (2005) is critical to the future of friendship research because of its specific emphasis on the dynamics of friendship, especially as they involve the balance between self and other. By looking at friendship dynamics per se as they relate to friendship processes, we will gain insight into friendship as a self-other management problem, particularly because the goals of this management task vary with the child's level of self-esteem. Indeed, a critical feature of the findings reported by Azmitia et al. is the bidirectional association between friendship and the self. Again, intrepid and inspired investigators will follow the path set by Azmitia et al. to see friendship in terms of self-other issues.

One final comment about the stuff of friendship is important and probably necessary. Peer interactions and relationships vary from one culture to another; cultures ascribe their own degree of significance to them (Rubin et al., in press). The stuff of friendships—the provisions, the processes, the balance of self and other—is likely to vary, for example, as a function of how much power is ascribed to kinship structures and of who makes primary decisions about what goes on outside the family. Moreover, since the defining features or characteristics of what it means to be adapted to one's social context differ across contexts, the impact on adaptation of particular characteristics of friendships is likely to vary also. In addition, within a culture, the effect of the peer system is likely to vary according to differences between children in provisions they obtain within their family. Indeed, a central tenet of the seminal views of Sullivan (1953) was that the developmental significance of friendship is higher for children whose relationships with parents was less optimal than it would be for other boys and girls. As French (in press) has shown, in cultures that ascribe considerable power or authority to the family system, the significance and meaning of friendship may differ substantially from the meaning of friendship in western cultures. It is conceivable that friendship may even be seen as a threat to the expected structure and influence of the family. Accordingly, friendship research needs to recognize the contextual variations in how friendship is constructed and in the role that friendship is given in children's lives.

Conclusion

Friendship deserves its place in the study of development. More than any other relational experience, it is part of our lives across the life span. In this way, the experiences of friendship in childhood and the skills and inclinations that we derive from these experiences are likely to have an enduring effect on our well-being throughout our lives. Theory from within and outside psychology has pointed to the complex nature of friendship and to its likely effects on how we function, how we think about ourselves, and how we deal with life's challenges. There is no doubt that friendship deserves to be recognized as a key developmental context.

Research on friendship has had a long and rich history. It has been with us since the earliest days of scientific study of human development. This interest has been especially keen in the past fifteen or twenty years. Yet, despite the activity in the literature on friendship and despite the rich theory related to it, research on friendship and the findings this research has produced have not been as powerful as one might expect. Our goal now is to reclaim the ideas and the concepts that gave rise to the interest in friendship as a key context or place where development happens. We propose in particular that we go back to the future and think, yet again and more carefully, about what we want to understand about friendship and what the goals of our studies should be. Akin to this effort is a need to see how friendship happens with respect to specific developmental needs and challenges. Insofar as friendship is seen as a source of need fulfillment, it has to be studied according to the needs or challenges that development poses. We propose that friendship must be understood according to the dialectic or interface between self and other. It is not just philosophers who point us in this direction. It is also the processes that we have identified as central to friendship—balance, conflict resolution, and intimacy, to name a few—that point to the importance of seeing friendship as a kind of experience that exists between two children and within each of them at the same time.

References

Azmitia, M., Ittel, A., & Radmacher, K. (2005). Narratives of friendship and self in adolescence. In N. Way & J. V. Hamm (Eds.), *The experience of close friendships in adolescence*. New Directions for Child and Adolescent Development, no. 107 (pp. 23–39). San Francisco: Jossey-Bass.

Badhwar, N. (1993). *Friendship: A philosophical reader*. Ithaca, NY: Cornell University Press.

Blatz, W. (1966). *Human security*. Toronto: University of Toronto.

Bukowski, W. M., Hoza, B., & Boivin, M. (1994). Measuring friendship quality during pre- and early adolescence: The development and psychometric properties of the friendship qualities scale. *Journal of Social and Personal Relationships, 11*, 471–484.

Cooley, C. H. (1909). *Social organization.* New York: Scribner.

French, D. (in press). Friendship in Indonesian and American children. *International Journal of Behavioral Development.*

Furman, W., & Robbins, P. (1985). What's the point: selection of treatment objectives. In B. Schneider, K. H. Rubin, & J. E. Ledingham (Eds.), *Children's peer relations: Issues in assessment and intervention* (pp. 41–54). New York: Springer-Verlag.

Hartup, W. W. (1996). The company they keep: Friendships and their developmental significance. *Child Development, 67,* 1–13.

Horney, K. (1950). *Neurosis and human growth.* New York: Norton.

Mead, G. H. (1934). *Mind, self, and society.* Chicago: University of Chicago Press.

Newcomb, A., & Bagwell, C. (1995). Children's friendship relations: A meta-analytic review. *Psychological Bulletin, 117,* 306–347.

Parker, J. G., & Asher, S. R. (1993). Friendship and friendship quality in middle childhood: Links with peer group acceptance and feelings of loneliness and social dissatisfaction. *Developmental Psychology, 29,* 611–621.

Rubin, K. H., Bukowski, W. M., & Parker, J. G. (in press). Peer interactions, relationships and groups. In W. Damon (Series Ed.) & N. Eisenberg (Vol. Ed.), *The handbook of child psychology* (6th ed.). New York: Wiley.

Sullivan, H. S. (1953). *The interpersonal theory of psychiatry.* New York: Norton.

Way, N., Gingold, R., Rotenberg, M., & Kuriakose, G. (2005). Close friendships among urban, ethnic-minority adolescents. In N. Way & J. V. Hamm (Eds.), *The experience of close friendships in adolescence.* New Directions for Child and Adolescent Development, no. 107 (pp. 41–59). San Francisco: Jossey-Bass.

Youniss, J., & Smollar, J. (1985). *Adolescent relations with mothers, fathers, and friends.* Chicago: University of Chicago Press.

WILLIAM M. BUKOWSKI *is professor in the Department of Psychology at Concordia University (Montréal, Québec), where he is also a member of the Centre de Recherche en Développement Humain.*

LORRIE K. SIPPOLA *is associate professor in the Department of Psychology at the University of Saskatchewan, in Saskatoon.*

PART FOUR

Self-Regulation of Emotion and Cognition

11

The executive attention network is involved in regulating emotions and cognitions, forming a neural basis for temperamental self-regulation. New brain imaging and molecular genetics methods can enhance our understanding of common mechanisms of self-regulation and individual differences in their expression.

Genes and Experience in the Development of Executive Attention and Effortful Control

Mary K. Rothbart, Michael I. Posner

Findings from neuroimaging research suggest that the physical basis of thoughts and emotions can be understood in terms of activation of anatomical areas organized into networks. These findings hold out the promise of integrating psychology—as proposed by Hebb (1949, 1966) decades ago—on the basis of the behavioral consequences of how network activation influences the behavior and mental processes of the person (for a recent and more detailed argument for the integration of psychology along these lines, see Posner & Rothbart, 2004). As we come to understand how brain mechanisms allow a child to control his or her own behavior, we have increased means to help the child overcome the many difficulties involved in self-regulation.

In this chapter, we describe new research strategies in the study of temperamental differences involved in effortful control and self-regulation as inspired by this integrated approach. We first describe our current understanding of the broad structure of temperament. Then we examine the functioning of the executive attention network, which has been shown to be related to the ability to regulate thoughts and feelings. This network involves a specific anatomy, including the anterior cingulate and prefrontal areas, modulated by dopaminergic input. Individual differences in the efficiency of the network are systematically related to particular genes. Finally, we examine how the training of attention in childhood might modify the network, and we consider how the interaction of genes and environment can influence the development of self-regulation.

Temperament

Temperament has been defined as constitutionally based individual differences in emotional, motor, and attentional reactivity and self-regulation, differences that demonstrate consistency across situations and relative stability over time (Rothbart & Derryberry, 1981). The term *reactivity* refers to the latency, rise time, intensity, and duration of responsivity to stimulation. The term *self-regulation* refers to processes that serve to modulate reactivity. In this chapter, we discuss executive attention networks in the human brain related to individual differences in temperamental self-regulation, which is termed "effortful control."

The concept of temperament stresses the links between biological mechanisms and their behavioral consequences. Over its long history of study, temperament has consistently been conceptualized in terms of the biology of the organism as understood at the time. In recent research, factor analyses of parent-report questionnaires have reliably extracted three or four broad temperament factors in childhood (Rothbart & Bates, 1998, in press). The first is *surgency,* or *extraversion,* with loadings from activity level, sociability, impulsivity, and enjoyment of high-intensity pleasure. The second is *negative affectivity,* with loadings from fear, anger or frustration, discomfort, and sadness; the third is *effortful control,* with loadings from attentional focusing and shifting, inhibitory control, perceptual sensitivity, and low intensity pleasure. Imaging studies have examined the neural systems underlying each of these systems (Canli et al., 2001; Ochsner, Bunge, Gross, & Gabrieli, 2002), but in this chapter we concentrate on effortful control in relation to development of the neural networks that support self-regulation.

Effortful control is the ability to inhibit a dominant response in order to perform a subdominant response, detect errors, and engage in planning. It develops in the second or third year of life and beyond (Rothbart, Posner, & Kieras, in press; Rothbart & Rueda, 2005). The development of executive attention skills underlies effortful control; as these skills develop individuals are more able to voluntarily deploy their attention, regulating their emotional and behavioral reactivity, including tendencies such as approach, fear, and anger (Posner & Rothbart, 2000; Rothbart & Bates, in press; Ruff & Rothbart, 1996). In situations where immediate approach is not allowed, for example, children can use their attention to resist temptation and delay gratification. When faced with a threatening stimulus, children can constrain their fear by attending to environmental sources of safety. Individual differences in effortful control allow children to suppress their more reactive tendencies, take in additional sources of information, and plan more efficient strategies for coping.

Findings indicate that individual levels of effortful control stay stable across childhood and adolescence (Rothbart & Bates, in press). For example, the number of seconds that a preschool child is able to delay while waiting to obtain a reward predicts parent-reported attentiveness and ability to concentrate in adolescence (Mischel, Shoda, & Peake, 1988). Low effortful control has been linked to development of children's externalizing problems and to depression (Rothbart & Bates, in press). Effortful control is also positively associated with empathy and development of conscience (Kochanska, 1995; Rothbart, Ahadi, & Hershey, 1994). As an aspect of temperament, effortful control allows flexible regulation of thought, emotion, and behavior.

Networks Underlying Executive Attention and Effortful Control

In our work with preschool children, we have shown that the ability to regulate conflict as measured by cognitive tasks is related to effortful control as measured by parent report (Gerardi-Caulton, 2000; Rothbart, Ellis, Rueda, & Posner, 2003). The Stroop conflict task and others appropriate for children have been shown in adult imaging studies to activate a specific network of brain areas, including the anterior cingulate and lateral prefrontal areas (Fan, Flombaum, McCandliss, Thomas, & Posner, 2003). For example, when conflict is induced between the direction of a central target arrow and the direction of surrounding flanker arrows in the Attention Network Task (ANT), children and adults show elevated reaction times, and adult studies indicate activation of the anterior cingulate. These and other findings (Botvinick, Braver, Barch, Carter, & Cohen, 2001) suggest that the cingulate monitors conflict between any two systems that are simultaneously activated and as such is part of a network underlying self-regulation (Botvinick et al., 2001; Rueda, Posner, & Rothbart, 2004). In support of this view, imaging studies of adults have shown that adjacent areas of the anterior cingulate are involved in regulation of cognition and emotion (Bush, Luu, & Posner, 2000). The anterior cingulate is also activated when adult subjects are asked directly to control their emotional reactions to positive and negative stimuli (Beauregard, Levesque, & Bourgouin, 2001; Ochsner, Bunge, Gross, & Gabrieli, 2002). These results suggest that a common brain network underlies the ability to resolve conflict and that important individual differences can be measured by self-report and by the efficiency of conflict regulation in cognitive tasks.

Genes

To understand both the common characteristics of this network and how the network differs among individuals, it is important to know which genes might be involved in network function. Animal studies have shown that dopamine is the principle modulator of the frontal areas important for self-regulation, and alleles of three dopamine genes have been reported to influence performance in conflict-related tasks such as the Stroop task and versions of the flanker task appropriate for young children (Diamond, Briand, Fossella, & Gehlbach, 2004; Fossella et al., 2002). Alleles of two of these genes have been shown in an imaging study to produce differential activation of medial and lateral frontal brain areas related to executive attention (Fan, Fossella, et al., 2003).

These studies demonstrate that at least part of the variability in the efficiency of executive attention is due to genetic differences, although the differences observed so far account for only a small part of the variance found in behavioral and imaging studies of attention. The genetic differences related to individual performance may nevertheless serve as clues to the genes involved in building the networks common to all individuals. Animal studies will allow further examination of the physical details involved in constructing such networks (Grandy & Kruzich, 2004).

Attention Training

There is evidence that educational experience can influence the functional anatomy of children following training. For example, studies of reading (Shaywitz et al., 2004; Temple et al., 2003) have demonstrated greater activation in phonological and visual word form areas following training in reading. It remains to be seen if these training effects involve changes in networks or reflect learning of a skill that can now better activate the networks. Even without knowing what lies behind these functional changes, it is already clear that imaging studies can result in a significant gain in design of interventions.

For children who suffer from attention deficit hyperactivity disorder (ADHD), training of attention and working memory have been found to produce improvements in concentration and in performance on general intelligence tests (Kerns, Esso, & Thompson, 1999; Klingberg, Forssberg, & Westerberg, 2002; Shalev, Tsal, & Mevorach, 2003). These studies all involved children age eight or older, with known difficulties in attention. In our recent studies, we have worked with normal four-year-olds to determine if attention training might serve as a potential contributor to preschool education (Posner, Rothbart, & Rueda, in press; Rueda, Posner, Rothbart, & Davis-Stober, 2004). Our studies were designed mainly to support the general concept of training attention and used small samples of children for limited periods of training.

We chose to focus on children age four because our previous studies had shown improvement in performance between four and seven years of age in the ANT (Rueda et al., 2004; Rueda, Posner, & Rothbart, 2004), which surveys the efficiency of performance related to attentional networks. The exercises in this research were patterned after those used to train rhesus macaque monkeys for space travel (Rumbaugh & Washburn, 1995). Exercises began with training the child to control the movement of an animated cat by using a joystick. The children were then able to control its movement to predict where an object would move, given its initial trajectory. Other exercises emphasized the use of working memory to retain information and the ability to resolve conflict. The exercises progressed from easy to difficult in seven levels, with the requirement that children perform each level correctly three times to proceed to the next level. Most of the children were able to complete the exercises within the five days allotted. For children who did not, we abbreviated some of the exercises to allow completion. Children seemed to enjoy the training, although they were clearly tired at the end of each half-hour to forty-minute session.

Children came to the laboratory on seven days for sessions conducted over a two- to three-week period. On the first and last days, effects of the training were assessed with the ANT; the K-BIT, a general test of intelligence (Kaufman & Kaufman, 1990); and a parent-report temperament scale (Children's Behavior Questionnaire, or CBQ; Rothbart, Ahadi, Hershey, & Fisher, 2001). During administration of the ANT, we recorded 128 channels of electroencephalograms (EEGs) to observe the amplitude and time course of activation of brain areas associated with executive attention in adult studies (van Veen & Carter, 2002). In our first study, we compared twelve randomly selected children who underwent this training with twelve children who took no training but came in twice for assessment. In our second experiment, we again used 12 four-year-olds, but the control group came on seven occasions and worked with interactive videos.

The findings showed significant impact from training. Five days is a minimal amount of training to influence the development of networks that change over many years. Nonetheless, we found a general improvement in intelligence in the experimental groups compared with the control groups, as measured by the K-BIT. This was primarily due to improvement of the experimental groups in performance on the nonverbal portion of the IQ test. Reaction time (RT) measures in the ANT proved to be highly unstable and of low reliability in children of this age; thus, we were not able to obtain significant improvement in the measures of the various networks, although overall RT did improve. We found that the experimental children produced smaller conflict scores after training than the control children, but this might have been due to differences in the pretest (despite random assignment).

Analysis of the brain networks using EEG recordings showed that the trained children's performance closely resembled performance by adults when they participated in the same conflict task. The N2 is a negative wave in the event-related EEG that, when recorded over frontal areas, has been shown to arise from activity in the anterior cingulate (Rueda, Posner, Rothbart, & Davis-Stober, 2004; van Veen & Carter, 2002). Both trained children and adults showed a larger N2 component of the event-related potential in trials where they were required to resolve conflict with the surrounding flankers. This was not true of the control children. We do not know if this change indicates merely that children performed the task better or that there was a change in the underlying network. However, the finding that differences in training generalized to an IQ test suggests a more general change in the network. We did no training of IQ, and the exercises in the K-BIT did not resemble any of the training tasks, yet in our studies and in related findings with older children (Klingberg et al., 2002) significant improvement in IQ was found.

The five-day training had no effect on parent reports of effortful control. As the number of children who undergo attention training increases, however, we will be able to examine aspects of children's temperament and genotype to help understand who might benefit from attention training. To this end, we are currently genotyping the children in an effort to examine candidate genes previously found to be related to the efficacy of executive attention. We are also beginning to examine the precursors of executive attention in even younger children, with the goal of determining whether there is a sensitive period during which interventions might prove most effective.

Conclusion

We hope in the future to have some preschools adopt attention training as a specific part of their curriculum. This would allow training over a more extensive time period, and it would allow evaluation of other forms of attention training, such as those that can occur in social groups (Mills & Mills, 2000). Although we do not yet know whether our specific program is effective, much less optimal, we believe that evidence for the development of specific brain networks during early childhood offers a strong rationale for sustained study to see if we can improve the attentional abilities of children.

The neural networks underlying thought and emotion are not limited to the specific skills of attention. In the future, increased understanding of how multiple networks develop and are shaped by experience may allow many aspects of socialization to benefit from training efforts. For example, through intervention research children's social adaptations and development of conscience might also be better understood.

More research will clearly be needed to tie together differences in behavior and the neural networks involved. We believe that future work in this field must rely on close coordination of methods, including parent- and child-report questionnaires, cognitive and emotional tasks that can be used to image human networks, and investigation of specific genes that may be related to the development of these networks. These approaches have made understanding of detailed mechanisms of temperament and their consequences for behavior in the real world a reasonable direction for developmental research in the coming years.

References

Beauregard, M., Levesque, J., & Bourgouin, P. (2001). Neural correlates of conscious self-regulation of emotion. *Journal of Neuroscience, 21*(18), 6993–7000.

Botvinick, M. M., Braver, T. S., Barch, D. M., Carter, C. S., & Cohen, J. D. (2001). Conflict monitoring and cognitive control. *Psychological Review, 108,* 624–652.

Bush, G., Luu, P., & Posner, M. I. (2000). Cognitive and emotional influences in the anterior cingulate cortex. *Trends in Cognitive Science, 4,* 215–222.

Canli, T., Zhao, Z., Desmond, J. E., Kang, E. J., Gross, J., & Gabrieli, J.D.E. (2001). An fMRI study of personality influences on brain reactivity to emotional stimuli. *Behavioral Neuroscience, 115,* 33–42.

Diamond, A., Briand, L., Fossella, J., & Gehlbach, L. (2004). Genetic and neurochemical modulation of prefrontal cognitive functions in children. *American Journal of Psychiatry, 161,* 125–132.

Fan, J., Flombaum, J. I., McCandliss, B. D., Thomas, K. M., & Posner, M. I. (2003). Cognitive and brain consequences of conflict. *NeuroImage, 18,* 42–45.

Fan, J., Fossella, J. A., Sommer, T., & Posner, M. I. (2003). Mapping the genetic variation of executive attention onto brain activity. *Proceedings of the National Academy of Sciences of the USA, 100,* 7406–7411.

Fossella, J., Sommer, T., Fan, J., Wu, Y., Swanson, J. M., Pfaff, D. W., et al. (2002). Assessing the molecular genetics of attention networks. *BMC Neuroscience, 3,* 14.

Gerardi-Caulton, G. (2000). Sensitivity to spatial conflict and the development of self-regulation in children 24–36 months of age. *Developmental Science, 3,* 397–404.

Grandy, D. K., & Kruzich, P. J. (2004). A molecular genetic approach to the neurobiology of attention utilizing dopamine receptor-deficient mice. In M. I. Posner (Ed.), *Cognitive neuroscience of attention* (pp. 260–268). New York: Guilford Press.

Hebb, D. O. (1949). *Organization of behavior.* Oxford, UK: Wiley.

Hebb, D. O. (1966). *A textbook of psychology.* Philadelphia: Saunders.

Kaufman, A. S., & Kaufman, N. L. (1990). *Kaufman brief intelligence test—manual.* Circle Pines, MN: American Guidance Service.

Kerns, K. A., Esso, K., & Thompson, J. (1999). Investigation of a direct intervention for improving attention in young children with ADHD. *Developmental Neuropsychology, 16,* 273–295.

Klingberg, T., Forssberg, H., & Westerberg, H. (2002). Training of working memory in children with ADHD. *Journal of Clinical and Experimental Neuropsychology, 24,* 781–791.

Kochanska, G. (1995). Children's temperament, mothers' discipline, and security of attachment: Multiple pathways to emerging internalization. *Child Development, 66,* 597–615.

Mills, D., & Mills, C. (2000). *Hungarian kindergarten curriculum translation.* London: Mills Production.

Mischel, W., Shoda, Y., & Peake, P. K. (1988). The nature of adolescent competencies predicted by preschool delay of gratification. *Journal of Personality and Social Psychology, 54,* 687–696.

Ochsner, K. N., Bunge, S. A., Gross, J. J., & Gabrieli, J.D.E. (2002). Rethinking feelings: An fMRI study of the cognitive regulation of emotion. *Journal of Cognitive Neuroscience, 14,* 1215–1229.

Posner, M. I., & Rothbart, M. K. (2000). Developing mechanisms of self-regulation. *Development and Psychopathology, 12,* 427–441.

Posner, M. I., & Rothbart, M. K. (2004). Hebb's neural networks support the integration of psychological science. *Canadian Psychology, 45,* 265–278.

Posner, M. I., Rothbart, M. K., & Rueda, M. R. (in press). Brain mechanisms of high level skills. In A. M. Battro, K. W. Fischer, & P. Léna (Eds.), *Mind, brain, and education.* Cambridge, UK: Cambridge University Press.

Rothbart, M. K., Ahadi, S. A., & Hershey, K. L. (1994). Temperament and social behavior in childhood. *Merrill-Palmer Quarterly, 40,* 21–39.

Rothbart, M. K., Ahadi, S. A., Hershey, K. L., & Fisher, P. (2001). Investigations of temperament at three to seven years: The children's behavior questionnaire. *Child Development, 72,* 1394–1408.

Rothbart, M. K., & Bates, J. E. (1998). Temperament. In W. Damon (Series Ed.) & N. Eisenberg (Vol. Ed.), *Handbook of child psychology, vol. 3: Social, emotional and personality development* (5th ed.). New York: Wiley.

Rothbart, M. K., & Bates, J. E. (in press). Temperament. In W. Damon, R. Lerner, & N. Eisenberg (Eds.), *Handbook of child psychology, vol. 3: Social, emotional, and personality development* (6th ed.). New York: Wiley.

Rothbart, M. K., & Derryberry, D. (1981). Development of individual differences in temperament. In M. E. Lamb & A. L. Brown (Eds.), *Advances in developmental psychology*, vol. 1 (pp. 37–86). Hillsdale, NJ: Erlbaum.

Rothbart, M. K., Ellis, L. K., Rueda, M. R., & Posner, M. I. (2003). Developing mechanisms of temperamental effortful control. *Journal of Personality, 71*, 1113–1143.

Rothbart, M. K., Posner, M. I., & Kieras, J. (in press). Temperament, attention, and the development of self-regulation. In K. McCartney & D. Phillips (Eds.), *The Blackwell handbook of early child development*. Oxford, UK: Blackwell.

Rothbart, M. K., & Rueda, M. R. (2005). The development of effortful control. In U. Mayr, E. Awh, & S. W. Keele (Eds.), *Developing individuality in the human brain: A tribute to Michael I. Posner* (pp. 167–188). Washington, DC: American Psychological Association.

Rueda, M. R., Fan, J., Halparin, J., Gruber, D., Lercari, L. P., McCandliss, B. D., et al. (2004). Development of attention during childhood. *Neuropsychologia, 42*, 1029–1040.

Rueda, M. R., Posner, M. I., & Rothbart, M. K. (2004). Attentional control and self-regulation. In R. F. Baumeister & K. D. Vohs (Eds.), *Handbook of self-regulation: Research, theory, and applications* (pp. 283–300). New York: Guilford Press.

Rueda, M. R., Posner, M. I., Rothbart, M. K., & Davis-Stober, C. P. (2004). Development of the time course for conflict resolution: An ERP study with 4 year olds and adults. *BMC Neuroscience, 5*, 39–51.

Ruff, H. A., & Rothbart, M. K. (1996). *Attention in early development: Themes and variations*. New York: Oxford University Press.

Rumbaugh, D. M., & Washburn, D. A. (1995). Attention and memory in relation to learning: A comparative adaptation perspective. In G. R. Lyon & N. A. Krasengor (Eds.), *Attention, memory, and executive function* (pp. 199–219). Baltimore: Brookes.

Shalev, L., Tsal, Y., & Mevorach, C. (2003). Progressive attentional training program: Effective direct intervention for children with ADHD. Paper presented at meeting of Cognitive Neuroscience Society, New York, Mar.

Shaywitz, B. A., Shaywitz, S. E., Blachman, B. A., Pugh, K. R., Fulbright, R. K., Skudlarski, P., et al. (2004). Development of left occipitotemporal systems for skilled reading in children after a phonologically-based intervention. *Biological Psychiatry, 55*(9), 926–933.

Temple, E., Deutsch, G. K., Poldrack, R. A., Miller, S. L., Tallal, P., Merzenich, M. M., et al. (2003). Neural deficits in children with dyslexia ameliorated by behavioral remediation: Evidence from functional MRI. *Proceedings of the National Academy of Sciences of the USA, 100*(5), 2860–2865.

van Veen, V., & Carter, C. S. (2002). The timing of action-monitoring processes in the anterior cingulate cortex. *Journal of Cognitive Neuroscience, 14*, 593–602.

MARY K. ROTHBART, *professor emerita at the University of Oregon, is a pioneer in the study of temperament and has developed measures for its study from infancy to adulthood.*

MICHAEL I. POSNER *is professor emeritus at the University of Oregon and was the founding director of the Sackler Institute for Developmental Psychobiology at the Weill Medical College in New York City.*

12

Research suggests that the development of emotional regulation in early childhood is interrelated with emotional understanding and language skills. Heuristic models are proposed on how these factors influence children's emerging academic motivation and skills.

Associations of Emotion-Related Regulation with Language Skills, Emotion Knowledge, and Academic Outcomes

Nancy Eisenberg, Adrienne Sadovsky, Tracy L. Spinrad

Recently there has been extensive discussion of the construct of emotion-related regulation, including its conceptualization, measurement, and relation to developmental outcomes. Definitions of the construct vary, but in general emotion-related regulation refers to processes used to manage and change if, when, and how one experiences emotions and emotion-related motivational and physiological states, and how emotions are expressed behaviorally. It is accomplished in diverse ways, notably through attentional and planning processes, inhibition or activation of behavior, and management of the external context.

Children's emotion-related regulation (labeled herein *regulation*) is increasingly viewed as a core skill relevant to many aspects of their socio-emotional and cognitive functioning. A recent Academy of Science committee concluded that "the growth of self-regulation is a cornerstone of early childhood development that cuts across all domains of behavior" (Shonkoff & Phillips, 2000, p. 3). Similarly, in a report funded by the National Institutes of Health concerning risk factors for academic and behavioral problems at the beginning of school, Huffman, Mehlinger, and Kerivan (2000) concluded that emotion regulation is critical for children's competence.

NEW DIRECTIONS FOR CHILD AND ADOLESCENT DEVELOPMENT, no. 109, Fall 2005 © Wiley Periodicals, Inc.

Like the members of the National Academy of Science committee, we believe that regulatory skills, including those involved in managing emotions and their expression, are central to many aspects of children's functioning. However, children's emotion-related regulation and other early developing abilities likely influence one another while they are emerging. In this chapter, we discuss links between children's regulation and two emerging skills: language and emotion understanding. In addition, we review findings on the relation of all three of these constructs to developmental outcomes that have infrequently been studied in relation to regulation: school readiness and academic skills. Finally, we propose a heuristic model for the interrelations among these variables, a model that has implications for research and for interventions with young people.

Emotion Regulation and Language.

Kopp (1989, 1992) suggested that language skills provide important tools for understanding and regulating children's emotions. Young children use language as a means to influence their environment. Specifically, children may use language in agentic self-managing talk, to communicate about social interactions, or to learn about appropriate ways to manage emotions. Consistent with this view, preschoolers' language skills have been positively correlated with their ability to use distraction in a frustrating situation (Stansbury & Zimmerman, 1999). In addition, language impairment is associated with boys' difficulty with emotion regulation (even for boys with age-appropriate abilities in other areas; Fujiki, Brinton, & Clarke, 2002). However, it is likely that emotion-related regulation and language affect one another, perhaps because better-regulated children elicit more complex language from others in their social environment (that is, adults may perceive well-regulated children as more attentive and advanced in their language skills). Consistent with the notion that language skills and regulation affect one another, infants' regulation (as evidenced by factors such as attention span and attentional persistence) predicts their language skills eight to nine months later (Dixon & Smith, 2000).

Regulation and Emotion Understanding.

Emotion-related regulation is associated with children's language skills and also their emotion understanding. Emotion understanding involves being able to successfully attend to relevant emotion-laden language and information in one's environment, identify one's own and others' experienced and expressed emotions, understand which emotions are appropriate given the circumstances, and recognize the causes and consequence of emotions. Regulation is probably integrally involved in the ability to focus on emotion-laden environmental cues in order to develop and fine-tune emotion understanding. Moreover, as suggested by Hoffman (1983), children who can avoid emotional overarousal likely learn more about emotion-related issues. Overaroused children are likely to attend to their own emotional experience and avoid an aversive situation, both of which are expected to reduce learning about others' emotions. Consistent with these ideas, preschoolers' level of regulation has predicted their understanding of emotion two years later (Schultz, Izard, Ackerman, & Youngstrom, 2001), and emotion understanding mediates the relations of regulation to adaptive social behavior (Izard, Schultz, Fine, Youngstrom, & Ackerman, 1999–2000; compare Lindsey & Colwell, 2003).

Conversely, emotion understanding may foster emotion regulation. Denham and Burton (in press) suggested that emotion understanding gives children a way to identify their internal feelings, which can then be made conscious. Such conscious emotional awareness allows children to immediately attach feelings to events, which can then facilitate successful and appropriate regulation (see also Gottman, Katz, & Hooven, 1997). Because emotion understanding involves not only verbal labeling of internal states but also knowledge about emotion-related processes and their causes and consequences, children can use their emotion understanding to choose effective regulatory tactics when upset (Liew, Eisenberg, & Reiser, in press). Researchers have found that children who are able to understand emotions, communicate about them, and learn and remember how to manage them are better able to regulate themselves (Denham & Burton, in press; Kopp, 1992).

Academics and Emotion Regulation.

Children's emotion regulation also has been conceptually linked to their academic success (Raver, 2002; Sanson, Hemphill, & Smart, 2004). For example, investigators have argued that emotion regulation (particularly attentional regulation and planning skills involved in executive attention) contributes directly to children's school readiness and academic competence because children who have difficulty controlling their attention and behavior are likely to be challenged when attempting to learn and focus in the classroom (Blair, 2002). In addition, as is discussed later, emotion regulation may contribute to children's motivation at school, which undoubtedly is linked to their academic performance.

Consistent with the view that regulatory processes affect academic performance, in the National Institute of Child Health and Human Development Early Childcare Research Network study (2003) attentional regulation at fifty-four months of age was positively related to high scores on achievement in reading and math, as well as linguistic ability (for example, auditory comprehension and expressive language). In another study, kindergartners' behavioral tendencies to self-regulate attention and teachers' ratings of second-graders' self-regulation were significant predictors of reading achievement scores (Howse, Lange, Farran, & Boyles, 2003). Similarly, youths' emotion regulation has been positively related to reading and math scores (Hill

& Craft, 2003), teacher-rated academic behavior skills (Hill and Craft), young adolescents' achievement scores, and teacher-rated academic competence, as well as with GPA when controlling for the effects of various cognitive variables (Gumora & Arsenio, 2002; Kurdek & Sinclair, 2000; Wills et al., 2001).

It is likely that the relation between children's regulation and academic competence is partly mediated by their social competence because socially competent children tend to do better in school. In a series of studies, Eisenberg and colleagues (as well as numerous others) have found that emotion regulation is related to children's social skills, popularity, and adjustment (Eisenberg, Fabes, Guthrie, & Reiser, 2000; Eisenberg, Smith, Sadovsky, & Spinrad, 2004). These skills in turn may be related to children's academic competence through their effect on children's social relationships at school, which appear to influence their motivation and performance at school (Furrer & Skinner, 2003). Consistent with an association between children's social and academic competence, Welsh, Parke, Widaman, and O'Neil (2001) found that young school children's positive (prosocial) behavior, social competence, and academic competence (that is, math and language grades and reported work habits) were reciprocally related. Similarly, peer competence (for instance, peer acceptance) in the early school years has been negatively related to concurrent and subsequent deficits in work habits, math and language or reading, negative school attitude, school avoidance, and underachievement during the first year or two of schooling (Ladd, 2003; O'Neil et al., 1997). Thus, if regulation affects children's social competence, then it likely also affects academic skills.

There is initial evidence that motivational factors such as liking school may at least partially mediate the relation between children's regulation and their academic competence. Valiente, Lemery, and Castro (2004) found such a relation with concurrent measures of the three constructs. Also consistent with such a mediated relation, children's reports of school liking and school participation have been positively related to classroom engagement, academic progress, and achievement (Buhs & Ladd, 2001; Ladd, Buhs, & Seid, 2000; Ladd & Burgess, 2001; Ladd, Kochenderfer, & Coleman, 1996).

The Model

To summarize thus far, the empirical literature, albeit limited in some respects, is consistent with the assertions that (1) there are relations among children's regulation, language skills, and emotion understanding; and (2) these variables have implications for children's academic motivation and performance. In Figure 12.1, we present a model of the proposed relations among young children's emerging language, emotion knowledge and understanding, and regulation. As is indicated in the model, language abilities likely promote emotion understanding and emotion-related regulation; moreover, emotion understanding may partly mediate the relation of language skills to

Figure 12.1. Hypothesized Interrelations of Children's Language Skills, Emotion Knowledge, and Emotion-Related Regulation over Time

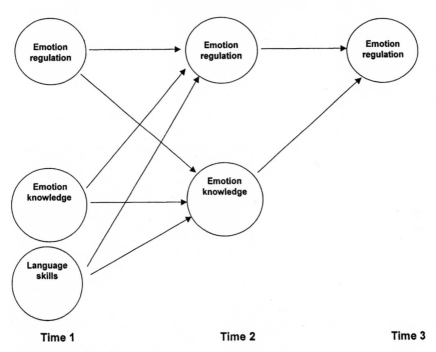

Time 1   Time 2   Time 3

emotion-related regulation. In support of the latter relation, verbal abilities have been correlated with children's emotion understanding (Cutting & Dunn, 1999; De Rosnay & Harris, 2002) and predict such understanding years later (Schultz et al., 2001). Children who are better able to communicate with others have more opportunity to learn about mental states, including emotion. In addition, as previously noted, children's emotion-related regulation likely affects their emotion understanding.

In Figure 12.2, we present a larger (yet simplified) heuristic model predicting academic outcomes. We suggest that children's emerging emotion-related regulation—as influenced by their emerging language and emotion understanding and knowledge—affects their academic motivation and skills both directly and through its effect on their social competence (including peer acceptance and social skills, which foster positive relations with teachers). There may also be additive main effects of regulation, emotion understanding, and language on social competence and academic outcomes. Lindsey and Colwell (2003) found that preschoolers' regulation and emotion understanding uniquely predicted their emotional competence with peers (they did not test for mediation). The complex

**Figure 12.2. Heuristic Model of Direct and Mediated Relations
of Emotion-Related Regulation, Language, and Emotion Knowledge
as Predictors of Children's Social Competence, Academic
Motivation, and Academic Skills**

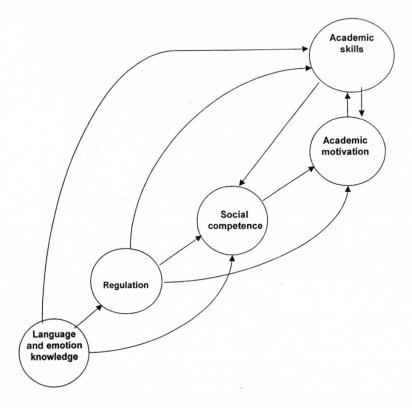

relations among language skills, emotion knowledge, and emotion-related
regulation that are depicted in Figure 12.1 are not fully depicted in Figure 12.2.

Research concerning the relation of regulation to other variables in the
model has already been discussed, as has research on the relation of social
competence to academic outcomes. In addition, in this model we suggest
that language abilities and emotion knowledge contribute to social competence and academic motivation and skills. Children who understand emotions well would be expected to know when to display or mask them and to
accurately interpret their own and others' emotions—skills that appear
to contribute to social competence. Fine, Izard, Mostow, Trentacosta, and
Ackerman (2003) hypothesized that low emotion knowledge affects the quality of children's social interaction, which in turn causes social alienation and

emotions such as anxiety, fear, and sadness, which further undermine social interaction. Consistent with this view, young children's emotion knowledge has been linked to their social competence (Denham & Burton, in press), and children's verbal skills (vocabulary, receptive language) have been found to predict social skills (Izard et al., 2001; Mostow, Izard, Fine, & Trentacosta, 2002), adjustment (Ackerman, Brown, & Izard, 2003; Fine et al., 2003; Olson & Hoza, 1993), and academic skills (Izard et al., 2001). Further, in support of the model there is evidence that emotion knowledge mediates the relations between children's verbal abilities and their social skills (and social skills did not predict emotion understanding; Mostow et al., 2002) and academic competence (Izard et al., 2001) years later. Thus, there is reason to expect language skills and emotion understanding to affect the development of social skills and adjustment and (on the basis of findings reviewed previously) for the latter to mediate relations of language skills and emotion knowledge with academic outcomes.

Developmental changes may affect the relations discussed in the model. For example, it is likely that language has a stronger effect on children's emotion understanding and regulation in the first two or three years of life, when basic and emotion-related language skills are rapidly emerging. Emotion understanding and regulation likely continue to have moderate effects on one another (as well as on social and academic outcomes) during the preschool and school years because both are improving considerably during this period of life. As children age, other factors, such as children's reputation with peers or peer history, may play an increasing role (along with regulation) in school liking and achievement. An important task for the future is to determine how age-related capacities and experiences affect the relations outlined in the models.

Conclusion

In this chapter, we briefly summarize relevant literature in an attempt to argue two major points: (1) emotion-related regulation is related to children's emotion knowledge, language skills, and academic competencies; and (2) it is useful to consider all these constructs, as well as social competence, when examining the relation of regulatory capacities to emerging academic performance and motivation. In addition, our heuristic model highlights the importance of mediating processes and bidirectional causality. We believe that it is important to consider a variety of emerging skills if one pursues interest in issues such as school readiness and academic motivation. Models of the sort we have presented may be useful when planning intervention programs for improving school readiness and success. We believe that targeting children's regulation and emotion understanding, as well as language skills, in intervention or prevention trials is likely to have a significant positive outcome for children's social and academic competence.

References

Ackerman, B. P., Brown, E., & Izard, C. E. (2003). Continuity and change in levels of externalizing behavior in school of children from economically disadvantaged families. *Child Development, 74,* 694–709.

Blair, C. (2002). School readiness: Integrating cognition and emotion in a neurobiological conceptualization of children's functioning at school entry. *American Psychologist, 57,* 111–127.

Buhs, E., & Ladd, G. W. (2001). Peer rejection in kindergarten: Relational processes mediating academic and emotional outcomes. *Developmental Psychology, 37,* 550–560.

Cutting, A., & Dunn, J. (1999). Theory of mind, emotion understanding, language, and family background: Individual differences and interrelations. *Child Development, 70,* 853–865.

Denham, S. A., & Burton, R. (in press). *Social and emotional prevention and intervention programming for preschoolers.* New York: Kluwer-Plenum.

De Rosnay, M., & Harris, P. L. (2002). Individual differences in children's understanding of emotion: The role of attachment and language. *Attachment and Human Development, 4,* 39–54.

Dixon, W. E., Jr., & Smith, P. H. (2000). Links between early temperament and language acquisition. *Merrill-Palmer Quarterly, 46,* 417–440.

Eisenberg, N., Fabes, R. A., Guthrie, I. K., & Reiser, M. (2000). Dispositional emotionality and regulation: Their role in predicting quality of social functioning. *Journal of Personality and Social Psychology, 78,* 136–157.

Eisenberg, N., Smith, C. L., Sadovsky, A., & Spinrad, T. L. (2004). Effortful control: Relations with emotion regulation, adjustment, and socialization in childhood. In R. F. Baumeister & K. D. Vohs (Eds.), *Handbook of self-regulation: Research, theory, and applications* (pp. 259–282). New York: Guilford Press.

Fine, S. E., Izard, C., Mostow, A., Trentacosta, C. J., & Ackerman, B. P. (2003). First grade emotion knowledge as a predictor of fifth grade self-reported internalizing behaviors in children from economically disadvantaged families. *Development and Psychopathology, 15,* 331–342.

Fujiki, M., Brinton, B., & Clarke, D. (2002). Emotion regulation in children with specific language impairment. *Language, Speech, and Hearing Services in Schools, 33,* 102–111.

Furrer, C., & Skinner, E. (2003). Sense of relatedness as a factor in children's academic engagement and performance. *Journal of Educational Psychology, 95,* 148–162.

Gottman, J. M., Katz, L. F., & Hooven, C. (1997). *Meta-emotion: How families communicate emotionally.* Hillsdale, NJ: Erlbaum.

Gumora, G., & Arsenio, W. F. (2002). Emotionality, emotion regulation, and school performance in middle school children. *Journal of School Psychology, 40,* 395–413.

Hill, N. E., & Craft, S. A. (2003). Parent-school involvement and school performance: Mediated pathways among socioeconomically comparable African American and Euro-American families. *Journal of Educational Psychology, 95,* 74–83.

Hoffman, M. L. (1983). Affective and cognitive processes in moral internalization. In E. T. Higgins, D. N. Ruble, & W. W. Hartup (Eds.), *Social cognition and social development: a sociocultural perspective* (pp. 236–274). Cambridge, MA: Cambridge University Press.

Howse, R. B., Lange, G., Farran, D. C., & Boyles, C. D. (2003). Motivation and self-regulation as predictors of achievement in economically disadvantaged young children. *Journal of Experimental Education, 71,* 151–174.

Huffman, L. C., Mehlinger, S. L., & Kerivan, A. S. (2000). *Risk factors for academic and behavioral problems at the beginning of school.* Bethesda, MD: National Institute of Mental Health.

Izard, C. E., Fine, S., Schultz, D., Mostow, A., Ackerman, B., & Youngstrom, E. (2001). Emotion knowledge as a predictor of social behavior and academic competence in children at risk. *Psychological Science, 12,* 18–23.

Izard C. E., Schultz, D., Fine, S. E., Youngstrom, E., & Ackerman, B. P. (1999–2000). Temperament, cognitive ability, emotion knowledge, and adaptive social behavior. *Imagination, Cognition, and Personality, 19,* 305–330.

Kopp, C. B. (1989). Regulation of distress and negative emotions: A developmental view. *Developmental Psychology, 25,* 343–354.

Kopp, C. (1992). Emotional distress and control in young children. In N. Eisenberg & R. A. Fabes (Eds.), *Emotion and its regulation in early development.* New Directions in Child Development, no. 55 (pp. 41–56). San Francisco: Jossey-Bass.

Kurdek, L. A., & Sinclair, R. J. (2000). Psychological, family, and peer predictors of academic outcomes in first- through fifth-grade children. *Journal of Educational Psychology, 92,* 449–457.

Ladd, G. W. (2003). Probing the adaptive significance of children's behavior and relationships in the school context: A child by environment perspective. In R. Kail (Ed.), *Advances in Child Development and Behavior, 31,* 43–103.

Ladd, G. W., Buhs, E., & Seid, M. (2000). Children's initial sentiments about kindergarten: Is school liking an antecedent of early classroom participation and achievement? *Merrill-Palmer Quarterly, 46,* 255–279.

Ladd, G. W., & Burgess, K. B. (2001). Do relational risks and protective factors moderate the linkages between childhood aggression and early psychological and school adjustment? *Child Development, 72,* 1579–1601.

Ladd, G. W., Kochenderfer, B. J., & Coleman, C. C. (1996). Friendship quality as a predictor of young children's early school adjustment. *Child Development, 67,* 1103–1118.

Liew, J., Eisenberg, N., & Reiser, M. (in press). Preschoolers' effortful control and negative emotionality, immediate reactions to disappointment, and quality of social functioning. *Journal of Experimental Child Psychology.*

Lindsey, E., W., & Colwell, M. J. (2003). Preschoolers' emotional competence: Links to pretend and physical play. *Child Study Journal, 33,* 39–52.

Mostow, A. J., Izard, C. E., Fine, S., & Trentacosta, C. (2002). Modeling emotional, cognitive, and behavioral predictors of peer acceptance. *Child Development, 73,* 1775–1787.

National Institute of Child Health and Human Development Early Child Care Research Network. (2003). Do children's attention processes mediate the link between family predictors and school readiness? *Developmental Psychology, 39,* 581–593.

Olson, S. L., & Hoza, B. (1993). Preschool developmental antecedents of conduct problems in children beginning school. *Journal of Clinical Child Psychology, 22,* 60–67.

O'Neil, R., Welsh, M., Parke, R. D., Wang, S. & Strand, C. (1997). A longitudinal assessment of the academic correlates of early peer acceptance and rejection. *Journal of Clinical Child Psychology, 26,* 290–303.

Raver, C. C. (2002). Emotions matter: Making the case for the role of young children's emotional development for early school readiness. *Social Policy Report, 16,* 3–18.

Sanson, A., Hemphill, S. A., & Smart, D. (2004). Connections between temperament and social development: A review. *Social Development, 13,* 142–170.

Schultz, D., Izard, C. E., Ackerman, B. P., & Youngstrom, E. A. (2001). Emotion knowledge in economically disadvantaged children: Self-regulatory antecedents and relations to social difficulties and withdrawal. *Development and Psychopathology, 13,* 53–67.

Shonkoff, J. P., & Phillips, D. A. (2000). *From neurons to neighborhoods: The science of early childhood development.* Washington, DC: National Academy Press.

Stansbury, K., & Zimmerman, L. K. (1999). Relations among child language skills, maternal socializations of emotion regulation, and child behavior problems. *Child Psychiatry and Human Development, 30,* 121–142.

Valiente, C., Lemery, K. S., & Castro, K. (2004). Children's effortful control and academic functioning: Mediation through school liking. Unpublished manuscript. Arizona State University, Tempe.

Welsh, M., Parke, R. D., Widaman, K., & O'Neil, R. (2001). Linkages between children's social and academic competence: A longitudinal analysis. *Journal of School Psychology, 30,* 463–481.

Wills, T. A., Cleary, S., Filer, M., Shinar, O., Mariani, J., & Spera, K. (2001). Temperament related to early-onset substance use: Test of a development model. *Prevention Science, 2,* 145–163.

NANCY EISENBERG is Regents' Professor of Psychology at Arizona State University.

ADRIENNE SADOVSKY is a postdoctoral research fellow in the Department of Psychology at Arizona State University.

TRACY L. SPINRAD is associate professor in the Department of Family and Human Development at Arizona State University.

13

Research patterns from the past three decades and several current directions of research are used to describe emerging trends in the study of cognitive development. These trends are discussed as moving the field into new areas, particularly biology, learning, and social context, and contributing to a more integrated understanding of psychological development.

With Eyes to the Future: A Brief History of Cognitive Development

Mary Gauvain

Predicting the future, even the near future, of theory and research in cognitive development is a formidable task. To do so in a relatively short chapter allows one to hit the highlights and forgo the all-too-important details, which makes the task a bit less daunting. To help set the stage for this chapter, a brief account of the recent history of the field is provided. Then the discussion turns to several areas of current research that follow up on some important themes in this history, specifically the biological bases of cognitive development (particularly in relation to emotional functioning), learning and cognitive development, and the contribution of the social context to intellectual growth.

This chapter has two aims. The first is to point out how some current areas of research are bringing together ideas about cognition and its development that have been percolating in the field for a while. The second is to suggest that these areas of research hold much promise for advancing our understanding of development in a way that integrates the cognitive, social, emotional, and biological aspects of growth. Such integration stands as a goal of the field at large, and it appears that research in cognitive development may play a central role in this formulation.

A Brief History

The past three decades have been witness to burgeoning interest in cognition and its development, which is clearly evident in one of the main sources in the field, the *Handbook of Child Psychology*. In the 1970 two-volume edition,

NEW DIRECTIONS FOR CHILD AND ADOLESCENT DEVELOPMENT, no. 109, Fall 2005 © Wiley Periodicals, Inc.

Carmichael's Manual of Child Psychology (third edition), there are twelve chapters on cognitive development; in the remaining seventeen chapters, there is scant mention of cognition. If we fast-forward to the 1983 four-volume set, the *Handbook of Child Psychology* (fourth edition), we find an entire volume devoted to cognitive development, and the discussion is largely restricted to this volume (save a few chapters on infant cognition that appear elsewhere). The most striking feature of this edition for our purposes is in the volume on social development: the subject index has nine brief entries pertaining to cognition, with a total of twenty-three pages on this topic out of the almost eleven hundred pages in the volume.

However, one chapter in the volume on cognitive development, on "Learning, Remembering, and Understanding" (Brown, Bransford, Ferrara, & Campione, 1983), is a harbinger of things to come. As the title of the chapter suggests, Brown et al. were more concerned with the processes of thinking than its products, a concern that has been increasingly central to the field since the chapter was written. Those authors were also prescient in their view that the field needs to move away from "academic cognition," in which thought and intelligent action are conceptualized as "relatively effortful, isolated, and cold" (p. 78) and therefore separate from other psychological states, toward examination of "hot cognition," in which thinking is connected to emotions, social processes, and other factors that compose the fabric of everyday functioning. Finally, Brown et al. encouraged researchers "to move this knowledge from the domain of laboratory lore to the domain of theory" because, as they cautioned, "if we do not, we may be ignoring some of the most important influences on development that exist. The emotional cannot be divorced from the cognitive nor the individual from the social" (p. 150).

If we fast-forward once more to the 1998 edition of the *Handbook* (fifth edition), a different picture of the field emerges. Coverage across the volumes is far less distinct than it was in the previous editions; most notably, cognition and cognitive development are all over the place. As in the 1983 edition, one volume is dedicated entirely to cognitive development, and all the traditional areas are represented (memory, perception, problem solving). However, now there are two chapters that concentrate on so-called hot cognition, one by Rogoff on "Cognition as a Collaborative Process" and the other by Flavell and Miller on "Social Cognition." Still other, even more dramatic changes appear in the three volumes that are not about cognitive development. In fact, every one of these volumes includes chapters on cognitive development. The volume on theories has chapters on knowledge development, cognitive science and the origins of thought, dynamics of action and thought, and culture and mind. The volume on practice has chapters on applications of research in cognitive development, including literacy, science and mathematics learning, and child testimony. Yet the most impressive change is found in the volume on social development, where four of the sixteen chapters are centrally concerned with cognitive processes, specifically emotional development and understanding, self-representations, motivation to succeed, and socialization processes, which includes cognitive perspectives on socialization such as parental beliefs and ethnotheories. The remaining chapters on social development all deal with cognition to some extent. As Eisenberg, the volume editor, notes in the Introduction: "cognitive processes of many sorts are being integrated into theory and research on diverse aspects of social and emotional development. This trend has resulted in richer conceptualizations of children and their social and emotional development, as well as of the socialization process" (p. 9).

The next edition of the *Handbook* is imminent, and according to the Table of Contents this trend will continue. Coverage of cognition and cognitive development is well ensconced throughout the volumes.

This brief look at history recounts two major trends in the field that are shaping current (and undoubtedly future) research. The first, more general, trend is increasing coverage and integration of cognition in all aspects of psychological development. The second, more specific, trend pertains to the relation of social and emotional processes and cognitive development, in terms of the cognitive nature of social and emotional behavior as well as the social and emotional nature of cognitive functioning. These trends have the potential to further a more integrated understanding of psychological development than existed just a decade ago. So, what are some current areas of research that reflect these particular trends? Let me highlight three broad directions of research that hold promise along these lines.

Three Current Research Directions

The first area of research concerns the biological underpinnings of cognitive functioning. There are several ways in which biology and cognitive development are currently studied: developmental cognitive neuroscience (Johnson, Munakata, & Gilmore, 2002), behavioral genetics (Plomin, DeFries, McClearn, & McGuffin, 2001), comparative and ethological approaches (Gottlieb, 1992), and evolutionary developmental psychology (Bjorklund & Pelligrini, 2002). Collectively, this research has offered (and will continue to offer) insight into basic cognitive functioning as well as how this functioning may relate in fundamental ways to the development of behavioral and social patterns and to the human evolutionary course. For instance, the social biases that have been revealed in research on face recognition in infancy (Pascalis, de Haan, & Nelson, 2002) and the emotional components of information processing in adolescence (Spear, 2000) illustrate how biologically based research may point directly to the intricate relation among the social, the emotional, and the cognitive over the course of development.

One area of biologically based research that seems especially promising for cognitive development focuses on the neural bases of emotions and how emotional development and regulation relate to the nature and course of cognitive growth (Davidson, 2000; Davidson, Jackson, & Kalin, 2000). Children's emotionality and regulatory capabilities help organize and support thinking and learning from the first year of life in a range of cognitive abilities (attention, behavioral inhibition, goal-directed planning, memory, and problem solving; Bell & Wolfe, 2004; Ruff & Rothbart, 1996). Research also suggests that emotions are important to learning in social context. Social learning situations that involve partners with strong emotional ties—such as parents and children, siblings, and friends—increase arousal, which in turn can enhance learning and memory. It is also known that adults adjust the support they give children on cognitive tasks according to some conception of the child's needs, which may reflect a perception of the child's abilities or emotionality. For example, research has shown that how parents approach instruction depends on their child's temperament or emotional state, part of which is the ability to regulate emotions in a new or stressful situation (Dixon & Smith, 2003; Perez, 2004). In short, emotional development and expression may regulate many of the opportunities for learning and cognitive development when children work on their own and with others.

A second promising area of study is learning. Although learning is a traditional topic in cognition, research on it has ebbed and flowed over the years as various learning theories have come into and fallen out of favor. As a result, many questions about learning and cognitive development remain to be answered. Fortunately, a resurgence of research on learning over the past decade has appeared in studies of problem solving, strategy development, and reasoning. For example, research on strategy development indicates that with age children have more strategies available, they develop more sophisticated strategies, and they use more efficient strategies that are adapted to the problem at hand (Siegler, 1996). There has also been extensive research on how children learn such academic subjects as mathematics, science, and reading, which has been vital to evaluating and revising educational practice (Bransford, Brown, & Cocking, 1999).

Despite increases in research on learning, the relation between learning and cognitive development—a topic that was of much interest to Piaget (1964) and Vygotsky (1978)—is still unclear. Many of the advances in the study of learning have relied on new techniques, notably microanalytical methods and computer simulations (Siegler, 2004). These techniques may prove useful for clarifying this relation. To this end, it is also important that research on learning is no longer restricted to the learning of laboratory-based cognitive tasks and academic skills. Learning approaches are increasingly seen in research on social development (as in the learning of social skills) and emotional development (such as the learning of display rules). Thus the process of learning is seen as a central mechanism by which children become competent cognitive, social, and emotional beings. Along these lines, the use of research techniques, especially the microgenetic method, to study processes of social and emotional development may be an important next step for research in this area. In addition, understanding of learning has stretched beyond the individual as researchers identify social processes that promote children's learning: observational learning, the social regulation of attention in infancy, deliberate efforts to transfer knowledge from more to less experienced partners, and social coordination during joint cognitive activity. This research suggests that social opportunities for children's learning appear in many forms and that cultures determine the frequency and manner with which these processes occur during childhood. A social approach to learning leads directly into the final area of research discussed, the social context of cognitive development.

A third promising area of research points to the social context as a critical component of cognitive development. The social context contributes to cognitive development in two ways. First, it determines what children think about and how children practice and adopt thinking. Second, it is the primary system through which children learn about the world and develop cognitive skills. In other words, cognitive development is an emergent property of social experience. During social interaction and other inherently social processes, such as participation in cultural practices (Rogoff, 2003), children have opportunities to participate intellectually in the world in a way that they cannot generate on their own (Vygotsky, 1978). These experiences lead to fundamental changes in how children think.

Older and more experienced members of society help shape intellectual development through the social interactions they have with younger, less experienced members, through the arrangements for learning that they furnish for children, and through the means of understanding the world that they reveal to children in social transactions. More experienced societal members also pass onto children the practices, skills, values, and goals of the community in which development occurs. Thus the process of cognitive development relies on the inherent link between the larger sociocultural context of development and the more immediate circumstances of individual growth. In other words, the sociocultural context is instantiated in local situations in how people interact, in the areas of mental functioning that are stressed and rewarded, and in the practices in which people engage. Accordingly, social processes organize the developing mind in a way that fits with the needs and aspirations of the community in which growth occurs.

This approach to cognitive development is functional in its theoretical orientation. It considers cognitive development as a socially mediated process creating an understanding of the world that enables a person to carry out meaningful and goal-directed actions. It also connects the individual mind with the minds of others (Nelson, 1996). For example, research has shown that adult-child conversation about past and current events supports cognitive development, especially memory development (Nelson & Fivush, 2000). This conversation is highly motivating because it is often about the children themselves and involves people who are familiar to the children. It communicates to children which events are worth learning and remembering (Snow, 1990) and therefore enhances children's attention to and memory for particular types of information and experience. It often relies on narrative structure, which influences how memories are constructed and recalled (Haden, 2003). Finally, conversation of this kind serves as a form of rehearsal (Hamond & Fivush, 1991). Children play an active role in this process of memory development. Research has shown that children's memory for an event is better when the event is talked about by the child and another person, such as the mother, than when the event is only talked about by another person or not discussed (Haden, Ornstein, Eckerman, & Didow, 2001). Research has also demonstrated that children use memory strategies in conversation with an unfamiliar adult similar to what was previously used with their mothers (Lange & Carroll, 2003), suggesting that parent-child conversation has implications for when children remember events on their own.

Concluding Thoughts

For developmental psychology as a whole to benefit from these three promising directions of research, it will be necessary to put findings from this research into a coherent understanding of psychological development. This effort will clearly need to be interdisciplinary. Each area of study is technical, requires mastery of a large literature, and deploys its own research techniques and levels of analysis. At present, there are some theoretical approaches, ones that emphasize interactive processes of change, that may be useful in this effort: dynamic systems theory (Thelen & Smith, 1994), ecological views (Bronfenbrenner & Morris, 1998), and sociocultural approaches (Rogoff, 2003).

The twenty-first century has barely begun, and the potential for understanding many of the questions that have been at the heart of developmental psychology for decades is enormous. The techniques of study, the sophistication of theories, the interdisciplinary nature of the field, and an abiding interest in asking hard questions about the human psychological experience will continue to serve the field well. The pitfalls are essentially the same ones developmentalists have faced all along: reductionism, overgeneralization of findings, theoretical orthodoxy, and limited representativeness of the participants or activities we study. Developmentalists have struggled with these issues for a long time, and though we will continue to do so we have the ability to spot them when we see them and try to confront them directly. The vexing issue of how to study and account for cognitive change remains a central concern. Understanding the processes or mechanisms that underlie cognitive development is a primary goal of the field and researchers will continue to strive to achieve this goal. The primary candidate for a mechanism of change that will surely receive attention over the next decade is the transaction between the biological and the social or experiential processes that promote and lead cognitive development.

It seems clear, given the brief history and areas of current research described here, that a cognitive approach will play an increasingly prominent role in the study of psychological development. Therefore, many of the advances in the near future will result from attempts to integrate biological foundations, processes of learning, and social experiences into some unified account of how children develop the enormous range of cognitive competencies that are characteristic of and essential to the species.

About a decade ago, there was a symposium at the Society for Research in Child Development titled Whither Cognitive Development? The concern expressed by the presenters was that the contribution of cognitive development to the field at large was in flux, perhaps even in jeopardy. Now, with a decade of hindsight on our side, it seems clear that the study of cognitive development has not "withered," but it definitely has transformed. The study of cognitive development has gotten more complex as well as increasingly integrated with the field as a whole. In this transformation lies great promise.

References

Bell, M. A., & Wolfe, C. D. (2004). Emotion and cognition: An intricately bound developmental process. *Child Development, 75,* 366–370.

Bjorklund, D. F., & Pelligrini, A. D. (2002). *The origins of human nature: Evolutionary developmental psychology.* Washington, DC: American Psychological Association.

Bransford, J. D., Brown, A. L., & Cocking, R. R. (1999). *How people learn: Brain, mind, experience, and school.* Washington, DC: National Academy Press.

Bronfenbrenner, U., & Morris, P. A. (1998). The Ecology of developmental processes. In W. Damon (Gen. Ed.) & R. M. Lerner (Vol. Ed.), *Handbook of child psychology, vol. 1: Theoretical models of human development* (pp. 993–1028) (5th ed.). New York: Wiley.

Brown, A. L., Bransford, J. D., Ferrara, R. A., and Campione, J. C. (1983). Learning, remembering, and understanding. In P. H. Mussen (Series Ed.) & J. H. Flavell & E. M. Markman (Vol. Eds.), *Handbook of child psychology, vol. 3: Cognitive development* (pp. 77–166) (4th ed.). New York: Wiley.

Damon, W. (1998). *Handbook of child psychology* (5th ed.). New York: Wiley.

Davidson, R. J. (2000). Affective style, psychopathology, and resilience: Brain mechanisms and plasticity. *American Psychologist, 55,* 1196–1214.

Davidson, R. J., Jackson, D. C., & Kalin, N. H. (2000). Emotion, plasticity, context and regulation: Perspectives from affective neuroscience. *Psychological Bulletin, 126,* 890–906.

Dixon, W. E., & Smith, P. H. (2003). Who's controlling whom? Infant contributions to maternal play behavior. *Infant and Child Development, 12,* 177–195.

Eisenberg, N. (1998). Introduction. In W. Damon (Gen. Ed.) & N. Eisenberg (Vol. Ed.), *Handbook of child psychology, vol. 3: Social, emotional, and personality development* (5th ed.). New York: Wiley.

Flavell, J. H., & Miller, P. H. (1998). Social cognition. In W. Damon (Gen. Ed.) & D. Kuhn & R. S. Siegler (Vol. Eds.), *Handbook of child psychology, vol. 2: Cognition, perception, and language* (5th ed.). New York: Wiley.

Gottlieb, G. (1992). *Individual development and evolution: The genesis of novel behaviors.* New York: Oxford University Press.

Haden, C. A. (2003). Joint encoding and joint reminiscing: Implications for young children's understanding and remembering of personal experiences. In R. Fivush & C. A. Haden (Eds.), *Autobiographical memory and the construction of a narrative self: Developmental and cultural perspectives* (pp. 49–69). Hillsdale, NJ: Erlbaum.

Haden, C. A., Ornstein, P. A., Eckerman, C. O., & Didow, S. M. (2001). Mother-child conversational interactions as events unfold: Linkages to subsequent remembering. *Child Development, 72,* 1016–1031.

Hamond, N. R., & Fivush, R. (1991). Memories of Mickey Mouse: Young children recount their trip to Disneyworld. *Cognitive Development, 6,* 433–448.

Johnson, M. H., Munakata, Y., & Gilmore, R. O. (2002). *Brain development and cognition: A reader* (2nd ed.). Oxford, UK: Blackwell.

Lange, G., & Carroll, D. E. (2003). Mother-child conversation styles and children's laboratory memory for narrative and nonnarrative materials. *Journal of Cognition and Development, 4,* 435–457.

Mussen, P. H. (1970). *Carmichael's manual of child psychology* (3rd ed.). New York: Wiley.

Mussen, P. H. (1983). *Handbook of child psychology* (4th ed.). New York: Wiley.

Nelson, K. (1996). *Language in cognitive development.* Cambridge, UK: Cambridge University Press.

Nelson, K., & Fivush, R. (2000). Socialization of memory. In E. Tulving & F.I.M. Craik (Eds.), *The Oxford handbook of memory* (pp. 283–295). London: Oxford University Press.

Pascalis, O., de Haan, M., & Nelson, C. A. (2002). Is face processing species-specific during the first year of life? *Science, 296,* 1321–1323.

Perez, S. M. (2004). Relations among child emotionality, mother-child planning, and children's academic adjustment and achievement in the first grade. Unpublished doctoral dissertation, University of California, Riverside.

Piaget, J. (1964). Development and learning. In R. E. Ripple & V. N. Rockcastle (Eds.), *Piaget rediscovered: A report of the conference on cognitive studies and curriculum development* (pp. 7–20). Ithaca, NY: Cornell University Press.

Plomin, R., DeFries, J. C., McClearn, G. E., & McGuffin, P. (2001). *Behavior genetics* (4th ed.). New York: Worth.

Rogoff, B. (1998). Cognition as a collaborative process. In W. Damon (Gen. Ed.) & D. Kuhn & R. S. Siegler (Vol. Eds.), *Handbook of child psychology, vol. 2: Cognition, perception, and language* (5th ed.). New York: Wiley.

Rogoff, B. (2003). *The cultural nature of human development.* New York: Oxford University Press.

Ruff, H. A., & Rothbart, M. K. (1996). *Attention in early development: Themes and variations.* New York: Oxford University Press.

Siegler, R. S. (1996). *Emerging minds: The process of change in children's thinking.* New York: Oxford University Press.

Siegler, R. S. (2004). Learning about learning. *Merrill-Palmer Quarterly, 50,* 353–368.

Snow, C. E. (1990). Building memories: The ontogeny of autobiography. In D. Cicchetti & M. Beeghly (Eds.), *The self in transition: Infancy to childhood* (pp. 213–242). Chicago: University of Chicago Press.

Spear, L. P. (2000). Neurobehavioral changes in adolescence. *Current Directions in Psychological Science, 9,* 111–114.

Thelen, E., & Smith, L. B. (1994). *A dynamic systems approach to the development of cognition and action.* Cambridge, MA: MIT Press.

Vygotsky, L. S. (1978). *Mind in society: The Development of Higher Psychological Processes.* Cambridge, MA: Harvard University Press.

MARY GAUVAIN *is professor of psychology at the University of California at Riverside. Her research focuses on cognitive development (in particular, planning skills and spatial thinking) in social and cultural context.*

INDEX

Back Issue/Subscription Order Form

Copy or detach and send to:

Jossey-Bass, A Wiley Company, 989 Market Street, San Francisco CA 94103-1741

Call or fax toll-free: Phone 888-378-2537 6:30AM —3PM PST; Fax 888-481-2665

Back Issues: Please send me the following issues at $29 each

(Important: please include series initials and issue number, such as CD99.)

_____

_____

_____

$ _____ Total for single issues

$ _____ SHIPPING CHARGES: SURFACE   Domestic   Canadian

First Item $5.00 $6.00

Each Add'l Item $3.00 $1.50

For next-day and second-day delivery rates, call the number listed above.

Subscriptions   Please ___ start ___ renew my subscription to *New Directions for Child and Adolescent Development* for the year 2 _____ at the following rate:

U.S.	___ Individual $90	___ Institutional $205
Canada	___ Individual $90	___ Institutional $245
All Others	___ Individual $114	___ Institutional $279

$ _____ Total single issues and subscriptions (Add appropriate sales tax for your state for single issue orders. No sales tax for U.S. subscriptions. Canadian residents, add GST for subscriptions and single issues.)

___ Payment enclosed (U.S. check or money order only)

___ VISA ___ MC ___ AmEx # _____ Exp. Date _____

Signature _____ Day Phone _____

___ Bill Me (U.S. institutional orders only. Purchase order required.)

Purchase order # _____

Federal Tax ID13559302   **GST 89102 8052**

Name _____

Address _____

_____

Phone _____ E-mail _____

For more information about Jossey-Bass, visit our Web site at www.josseybass.com

Other Titles Available in the
New Directions for Child and Adolescent Development Series
Reed W. Larson and Lene Arnett Jensen, Editors-in-Chief
William Damon, Founding Editor-in-Chief

**NEW DIRECTIONS FOR
CHILD AND ADOLESCENT DEVELOPMENT
IS NOW AVAILABLE ONLINE AT WILEY INTERSCIENCE**

What is Wiley InterScience?

Wiley InterScience is the dynamic online content service from John Wiley & Sons delivering the full text of over 300 leading scientific, technical, medical, and professional journals, plus major reference works, the acclaimed Current Protocols laboratory manuals, and even the full text of select Wiley print books online.

What are some special features of Wiley InterScience?

Wiley Interscience Alerts is a service that delivers table of contents via e-mail for any journal available on Wiley InterScience as soon as a new issue is published online.
EarlyView is Wiley's exclusive service presenting individual articles online as soon as they are ready, even before the release of the compiled print issue. These articles are complete, peer-reviewed, and citable.
CrossRef is the innovative multi-publisher reference linking system enabling readers to move seamlessly from a reference in a journal article to the cited publication, typically located on a different server and published by a different publisher.

How can I access Wiley InterScience?

Visit http://www.interscience.wiley.com.

Guest Users can browse Wiley InterScience for unrestricted access to journal tables of contents and article abstracts, or use the powerful search engine.
Registered Users are provided with a *Personal Home Page* to store and manage customized alerts, searches, and links to favorite journals and articles. Additionally, Registered Users can view free online sample issues and preview selected material from major reference works.
Licensed Customers are entitled to access full-text journal articles in PDF, with select journals also offering full-text HTML.

How do I become an Authorized User?

Authorized Users are individuals authorized by a paying Customer to have access to the journals in Wiley InterScience. For example, a university that subscribes to Wiley journals is considered to be the Customer. Faculty, staff and students authorized by the university to have access to those journals in Wiley InterScience are Authorized Users. Users should contact their library for information on which Wiley journals they have access to in Wiley InterScience.

ASK YOUR INSTITUTION ABOUT WILEY INTERSCIENCE TODAY!